# SMALL ENOUGH TO CO

# SMALL ENOUGH
# TO CONQUER THE SKY


## JIM DENYER
### 'MR NEWCASTLE AIRPORT'


*A biography of a flier*
*by*
# John Sleight


Newcastle upon Tyne
City Libraries & Arts, 1993

## By the same author

*Women on the March*, 1986
*One way Ticket to Epsom*, 1988
*The City Centenary; 100 years of Golf at City of Newcastle GC*, 1991

British Library Cataloguing in Publication Data: A catalogue record for this book is available from the British Library

ISBN: 1 85795 085 2

This book is dedicated to Mary Denyer

# CONTENTS

# ILLUSTRATIONS

1   Jim Denyer as a baby.
2   The young schoolboy at primary school.
3   Experienced RAF fliers being trained as Instructors.
4   Commissioned as a Pilot Officer.
5   Alan Taylor.
6   Pilot Denyer in the cockpit of his Dakota during the Berlin airlift.
7   Jim Denyer's Mosquito.
8   1954. The first radar set at Newcastle Airport.
9   Auster Autocrat, the plane that brought him to victory in 1956.
10  Winning the King's Cup in 1956.
11  Jim Denyer with Allan Irwin and Alec Imrie.
12  Jim's Tiger Moth.
13  After winning the Norton Griffiths International Trophy.
14  Double win for Jim in the 1958 air races.With his sons.
15  After winning the 1958 King's Cup.
16  Pilots of the municipal flying school.
17  The Canadair aircraft dumped at Newcastle Airport.
18  Jim Denyer, Lord Thomson, T. Dan Smith.
19  Ella Fitzgerald arriving at Woolsington in the 1960s.
20  Jim Denyer with the Lord Lieutenant (the late Duke of
    Northumberland), Prince Philip and the Queen.
21  At the controls of a Dakota preparing for take-off.
22  Jim Denyer awarded the 'Geordie Passport'.
23  Newcastle Airport Security Police make a presentation to Jim.
24  'Queen of the Skies' Amy Johnson visits Cramlington Aerodrome.
25  P. Forsyth Heppell.
26  Philip Whaley Heppell.
27  Rhoda Fairbairn, née Heppell.
28  The late Sheila Scott.
29  An outstanding woman pilot of the 1930s, Winifred Brown.
30  Damaged Miles Messenger.
31  Jim Denyer in the cockpit.
32  Jim Denyer with John Donnelly at his retirement.
33  The Managing Director and his successor, Trevor Went.
34  A high-wing monoplane with a farewell message.
35  The first airport licence, issued 23 July 1936.
36  John D. Irving at Woolsington.
37  The RAF flypast at the official opening 26 July 1935.
38  An aerial view of the early airport.
39  Summer 1935, the entrance to the airport.
40  Newcastle Municipal Aerodrome's first fire engine.

# IN COLOUR

# INTRODUCTION

## THE MAN WHO WAS BORN TO FLY

This book sets out to recount the story of Jim Denyer who, though hailing from a humble background, reached out for the sky and plucked some of its richest prizes.

The gifted pilot and later dynamic airport manager, became well-known in North East England, even the length and breadth of the country where civil aviation and airports were concerned. It is no exaggeration to say that after establishing himself at Woolsington he became a household name to many thousands in the region. So much so, that he became known as 'Mr Newcastle Airport.' That sobriquet was not undeserved as the evidence submitted on the following pages will show.

James Henry Denyer, Londoner, though Geordie by adoption,was the kind of irrepressible character who, picking out the goal ahead, went for it with determination and verve; the kind of man who would not take 'No' for an answer; who could hold his own with bureaucrats and politicians alike. On matters concerning Newcastle International Airport, he was a straight talker and tough negotiator.

His great love in life, family apart, was flying; he was never happier than when he was seated at the controls of an aircraft, preparing for take-off. He piloted so many different kinds of planes in fifty years of flying that his log-books resemble aviation dictionaries.

During his working life he crowded several flying careers into one—war-time night-fighter pilot, peace-time instructor in the Royal Air Force, flying club chief instructor, racing pilot and airport managing director. His contribution to the continued success of Newcastle Aero Club was not small: during one early period, he was instrumental in saving the flying side from closing down.

In fact the airport and the Aero Club provided the inspiration for his long working life. There is little he did not know about the historic background of those two organisations. To sit down with 'J.D.' in the Aero Club and over a 'jar' listen to the anecdotes and experiences come tumbling out was to travel along some of the absorbing paths of local aviation history.

Vivid stories of the Newcastle aviation pioneers came to light, as well as some of the trials and tribulations that both club and airport faced over the years. Like all good story tellers, his tales were garnished with a touch of wry humour.

He took great pride from many achievements at Woolsington; two that gave him special satisfaction were the creation of a modern international airport from a grassy field and a few huts, and his ability to hold a commercial pilot's licence for forty years, the only airport manager in England to do so.

His life-time of service was not confined to the North East, although he held a number of honorary posts here, not least two associated with the activities of the Air Training Corps. Nationally, he was linked to some of the most prestigious bodies in British aviation, including the Chartered Institute of Transport, the Airport Operators' Association and the Royal Aeronautical Society, the highest body in aviation in this country.

The one thing that one could say unequivocally about Jimmy Denyer is that he was a 'character'. To people who did not know him, he might have come over at first meeting as rather a caustic customer, though underneath, he was always a thoughtful and caring man; there is plenty of evidence to suggest that through the years, 'J.D.' helped a good many people in need without others getting to know about it.

His services to aviation and the North East region have not gone unrecognised: he was a recipient of the Order of the British Empire, and also received an Hon. MA from the University of Newcastle.

James Henry Denyer, a pre-eminent aviator, the architect of today's modern Newcastle International Airport, will long be remembered.

He died peacefully at his home in Darras Hall, Ponteland, Northumberland at one minute past midnight on 4 March 1993, aged sixty-nine, after a terminal illness which began in January, 1992.

It was the end of an era for Newcastle International Airport, his life's work.

Many tributes were paid to him, including the following:

Councillor Joe Hattam, chairman of the Airport Board: 'Jim has left us a diamond in the crown of the Northern Region. His efforts made it possible for this region to become a region of growth.'

Mr Trevor Went, Managing Director of the Airport: 'Jim's determination and tenacity was a major factor in providing the region with a prime transportation asset.'

Staff at Newcastle Airport: 'His strong, engaging presence and personality will be missed by all.'

Sir Colin Marshall, chairman of British Airways, who had known Jim Denyer for thirty-two years: 'I had considerable respect for Jim and his achievements, as well as his unstinting support for the development of Newcastle Airport. We will all miss him. This country and our industry is that much worse off for his loss.'

Wing Commander P. Hodgson, No. 29 (F) Squadron, Royal Air Force, Coningsby, Lincolnshire: 'No. 29 (F) Squadron greatly values its links with former Squadron members...the name of Jimmy Denyer is part of our Squadron history, which will be passed on to further generations of Fighter crews.'

## CAREER DETAILS

**Royal Airforce 1940-51**
With No. 29 Squadron, Fighter Command
No. 38 Group Transport Command
Training Command

**Newcastle upon Tyne Aero Club**
Chief Flying Instructor 1951-52
Manager, Municipal Flying School
Club President

**National Air Racing**
King's Cup winner 1956 and 1958
Norton-Griffiths International Challenge Trophy winner 1955 and 1959
Runner up British air racing championship 1955
Grosvenor Challenge Trophy winner, 1957
Lord Grosvenor Trophy Winner 1958

**Newcastle International Airport**
Airport Director 1952-1989
Newcastle upon Tyne Aero Club 1951-1993

This book also contains a history of Newcastle Aero Club, one of Britain's pioneering light aeroplane clubs, founded in 1925. Jim Denyer, longest serving President, was still Club President at the time of his death in March 1993.

# Chapter I

## FLYING WITH A WAR-TIME SQUADRON

## TROUBLE OVER GERMANY

RAF night-fighter pilot Jim Denyer, all of twenty-two years, walked briskly from the squadron briefing room across the tarmac towards his powerful, twin-engine Mosquito aircraft with its lethal fire-power and lightning speed.

It was 1945, the final year of World War II. Jim and his navigator and friend, Vivian Kellard, were making last minute checks before taking off from a Kent airfield on another sortie against the enemy.

Everything seemed to be in good order with the Mosquito 30, and despite the danger that threatened war-time missions over enemy territory, including hostile anti-aircraft fire, Jim felt that life was good. He was flying with the crack No. 29 Mosquito Squadron, and backed up in his own machine by a reliable navigator and radar operator.

He was also fortunate to be sitting at the controls of the 'wonder aircraft' of the war, the beautifully crafted, all-wood aeroplane that could outpace the earliest Spitfires. He knew that the sting from this Mosquito was deadly enough to out-shoot most enemy aircraft, possessing an armoury of four 20mm cannon.

Away from the toils of war, he had had the good fortune to meet an attractive young girl from Newcastle upon Tyne who was to become his wife.

After completing pre-flight checks, pilot Denyer signed his readiness; the twin engines of the machine burst into life, chocks were pulled away and the aircraft slowly approached the runway ready for take-off. Next minute, the fighting machine was roaring into the clouds with Viv Kellard setting a course for Germany.

The flight over the channel was uneventful. As they approached enemy territory they caught sight of smoke explosions in the sky; the German ack-ack gunners were at work, though nothing impeded the progress of the Mosquito, the twin Rolls-Royce Merlin engines pushing it smoothly forward at a speed approaching 400 miles per hour. After some time, the navigator's voice came over the plane's intercom to report that they had crossed the Belgian border and were now over Germany; Aachen to be precise.

It was at that moment that an oil-pressure warning appeared on the control panel in the cockpit, revealing a major fault in the starboard engine which began excessive rough-running. In a matter of a few seconds the plane lost half its power. Warrant Officer Pilot Denyer summed up the size of the problem: he was flying among hills and full power was needed to lift the heavy aircraft clear of the rising ground.

He had no choice, he had to put down; to crash-land on a suitable field, or, if he was lucky, to find a disused runway which would ensure a safer landing. To lighten the aeroplane, he opted to release the 100 gallon drop-tanks under the wing. When he pressed the release button, the mechanism jammed and failed to release them. Desperately searching for somewhere to land, he spotted a German airfield with what appeared to be a temporary metal runway. There were no signs of activity so Jim told his navigator: 'We are going in.' As the RAF flier manoeuvred his faulty machine onto the approach path, he was aware of the dangers—on either side of the runway he could see crashed German aircraft and other debris.

Then he had to grapple with another emergency: flying on only one engine had reduced the hydraulic pressure on the undercarriage system, which was slow to come down. On the final approach, Viv Kellard had to quickly work up the emergency handpump to help the undercarriage down. In the end, it was close thing: a split second before the damaged plane hit the runway the undercarriage warning light changed to green. Mosquito and crew were down in one piece...

Landing in enemy territory, they had no time to lose in seeking cover. Pilot and navigator leapt out of the Mosquito into a nearby ditch. The RAF pilot had had no time to think about his imminent wedding to his pretty eighteen-year-old fiancée, Mary Graham, from Newcastle. Though later the thought flashed through his mind—might he be missing from his own wedding?

For some time, the airmen lay hidden at the side of the road. Jim takes up the story: 'Eventually, we heard vehicles approaching. Peering out from the ditch was a sight for sore eyes—approaching was an Allied convoy led by American Jeeps. The Commander told me, 'You were lucky you did not have to land yesterday, there was a hell of a battle with the Germans for that airstrip.'

The urgent task ahead for the RAF crew was to get back to the United Kingdom and their own fighter Squadron, which forced them to abandon their Mosquito. Helped by Allied Forces transport, they travelled through Aachen on to Brussels where they hitched a lift with the American crew of a DC-3.

Despite Warrant Officer Denyer's father being informed that his son was missing, both Denyer and Kellard were able to rejoin 29 Squadron at its Manston, Kent, base within days. Without further ado, the wedding of James Henry Denyer, night-fighter pilot from Peckham, and Mary Graham, seamstress (Fenwick's) from Newcastle upon Tyne was celebrated.

Although the happy couple could not have known it then, that marriage partnership would take them six years later from their life in a RAF Station in the South to a new career with Newcastle Aero Club.

The saga of J.H. Denyer and the creation of a modern Newcastle Airport owed its beginnings to a chance meeting with Mary Graham at an all-rank dance at RAF Woolsington in 1943. The Air Force had taken over Newcastle Corporation's airfield at Woolsington at the start of the war. When the couple took to the floor for their first dance, Jim was then a twenty-year-old Sergeant Pilot, and Mary from Heaton, Newcastle was sixteen. Only the fortunes of war could bring together a young Cockney airman and a Geordie lass from the Tyne.

The first chapter in the story of how Jim Denyer became the Commandant of the local airport was written in 1950. The Denyers were on holiday in Newcastle and a casual call at the old Woolsington airfield he knew during war-time resulted in the offer of the job of Chief Flying Instructor to the Aero Club. Just one year later, and out of the blue, he was appointed Director of Newcastle Airport.

Before war broke out in 1939, he was a teenager with no interest in flying and aviation. At the beginning of hostilities, the Battle of Britain and the feats of the famous 'Few' inspired a desire to join the Royal Air Force. His wish was to come true.

The son of parents who lived in Peckham, London he was born in a Westminster hospital in 1923. James Edward Denyer, a long distance lorry driver, and Lavinia Florence, had three children of whom Jim was the eldest. He remembers the family unit as a happy home, where Mrs Denyer bore the brunt of bringing up the children as his father was so often working away.

As a school boy attending a London primary school he showed promise, winning two scholarships: one to London's Crofton Park Central School, and the other to Dartford Technical College. Away from his studies, he showed some prowess at football and cricket, though swimming was his favourite sport. He was still a boy when his parents moved their home from London to Kent. At sixteen he left college and started work with the Vidor Battery Co, of Burndeps, Erith, Kent. After only six months, he left to become an apprentice sheet metal worker, and panel beater, at the Royal Arsenal Co-operative Society at Charlton. His ambition was to become an engineering draughtsman but, like thousands of other young men in 1939, his future would be dictated by the outbreak of the Second World War.

However, the first uniform the sixteen-year-old Jim donned was not Air Force blue but Army khaki. As a member of the Local Defence Volunteers (Home Guard) he helped to defend the Commonwealth Buildings on the Thames in 1939 against any surprise attack. He also served as an Air Raid Warden.

Inspired by the exploits of Battle of Britain pilots, and shuddering at the thought of being called up by the Army (he hated marching), Jimmy Denyer decided to volunteer. He got on his bike and cycled to the nearest RAF recruiting office which happened to be in a public house at Eltham.

As he walked through the door of the office, a RAF officer said 'Good morning, Sir.' Jim carries on the story: 'I turned round to see who he was referring to and seeing nobody else, realised it was me! He asked me if I wanted to fly and as I thought that flying meant no marching I said "yes".'

Passing the standard entry test for air crew (category pilot, navigator, bomb-aimer) he was disappointed to be told that because he was too young to fly he would be placed on Deferred Service. And in any case, because of his short stature (he was five feet four inches tall), he would have to undergo a leg-length test at RAF Uxbridge to confirm that he could reach the controls of an aircraft.

He recalls his visit to Uxbridge with some glee: 'I arrived on the given day, presented my chit at the guardroom, and was taken by a Flight-Sergeant to a parked Spitfire. I climbed into the cockpit and sat on the bucket seat on cushions in lieu of a parachute. On the order "Rudder Left" I was to push the appropriate control with my foot; and on "Rudder Right" repeat the exercise. The examiner shouted out the instructions, saw the rudders move and gave me the thumbs up. I climbed out of the cockpit highly delighted. What the RAF Flight-Sergeant did not know was that I could hardly reach the controls. I had to stretch like mad for a split second to move them with my toes.

'After that and when I began serious flying training followed by missions against the enemy, I flew sat on a parachute with a cushion tucked behind me in the cockpit. That was my permanent *modus operandi!*'

He went on to train as a night-fighter pilot, specialising in low-level attack. Coming through the war unscathed, he elected to continue his RAF Commission in 1945. If he thought that life in a peace-time Air Force, with the privileges and perks due to an officer was going to be 'a piece of cake', he soon got a rude awakening.

It came as a result of Russia's occupation of Eastern Germany after the war and, later, in 1948 creating a international crisis by cutting off Berlin. By locking that stranglehold on Berlin, Russia expected the people of that great city to capitulate to them. That was the last thing that Berliners wanted, and as the crisis blew up the Allies decided to supply the city by air as all other routes were blocked.

That placed the RAF on a war footing once again, and the 'miracle' of the Berlin airlift began. From a pilot's point of view, supplying Berlin was to turn out to be a most dangerous mission, an experience that was soon to be the lot of Flying Officer Denyer. Access to the Berlin airfields was via narrow air corridors created by the Russians who maintained strong fighter presence on either side. Flying heavily laden cargo planes in huge numbers, day and night, stacked in the sky like sardines in a tin, was a risky business for the Allied pilots. Any British, French or American aircraft straying out of one of the narrow corridors invited retaliation by Russian Yak fighters, reactions which could only be defined as acts of war.

Nevertheless, despite the Russians and atrocious winter weather, food, fuel and other vital necessities were successfully flown into Berlin and the people survived. The Berlin airlift was a very frightening experience, worse than doing a tour of operations in war-time was J.D.'s view. He flew through most of the airlift in 1948 and 1949, and retains flying memories that he will never forget.

Rather less challenging, though not without its pressures, were RAF postings to Parachute Training Schools at Ringway and Upper Heyford, Oxford, where he piloted jump planes for the Parachute Regiment. Later, and still in the RAF, he became a flying instructor, teaching pupil pilots.

He had already served six years in the peace-time Royal Air Force when fate stepped in and radically changed his life. It happened in a most unusual way, in fact when he was on holiday with his wife Mary, and twin sons, Vivian and Michael, on Tyneside in 1950. He was seized with the notion of taking a nostalgic look at old RAF Woolsington which he knew from war-time days. When he arrived at the airfield he, by chance, walked into an aircraft hangar belonging to Newcastle Aero Club. An engineer approached him and asked him if he wanted to learn to fly! The engineer was soon filled in with a summary of J.D.'s extensive flying experience, only for him to reply that there was a vacancy in the Aero Club for a Chief Flying Instructor. Might he be interested in taking the post? After the necessary interviews, he took the job, the start of a career at Woolsington in 1951, which was to last for nearly forty years. Establishing himself as the Aero Club's CFI, he was then offered the post of Commandant of the Airport which he accepted in 1952. He was about to embark on the biggest challenge of his life—transforming the little grass airfield called Woolsington, with its old wooden huts, into the International Airport for the North that we know today.

# Chapter II

## EARLY DAYS AT WOOLSINGTON

## TALES OF 'BIGGLES ' AND BARNSTORMING AVIATORS

When James H. Denyer returned to Woolsington in 1951 to be interviewed for the post of Chief Flying Instructor to Newcastle Aero Club, little had changed on the little rural airfield since the end of the Second World War. The view that greeted him would not have looked out of place in a 'Biggles' flying field film set, where pilots flew in cockpits wearing 'Irvin' jackets, leather helmets and goggles and Tiger Moth bi-planes buzzed around.

The Aero Club and the airport shared three hangars, one built by Newcastle Corporation before the war, and the others erected by the Royal Air Force during war-time There was an old wooden control tower standing on stilts; a collection of old wooden huts; and a grassy strip that served as a runway. It was a tranquil aviation scene set in picturesque Northumberland countryside.

J.D. (the name by which he was known to all) was interviewed by the Aero Club Committee led by an outstanding local aviator called J.D. Irving. Denyer told the Committee that his career in the RAF was finely balanced (he was a Flight Lieutenant and top category flying instructor) but if the post was offered he believed that he could obtain his release. The post was offered and he submitted a request to leave the peace-time Air Force: 'My release was not straight-forward but helped by J.D. Irving, who had friends at the Air Ministry, my release papers came through without too much delay,' he recalled.

So in the summer of 1951 he became Chief Flying Instructor at Newcastle, little knowing that he would remain at the Woolsington Airfield for almost forty years. On his first day at the Aero Club, he was surprised to see that the first member to take up an aeroplane was seventy years old! J.D. remembers the occasion well:

'I was met at the airfield by George Williamson, the club treasurer, and as we walked down to the apron, I saw an expensive looking vintage car draw up between the hangars and an elderly gentleman alight dressed in leather flying jacket, helmet and gauntlet gloves. He walked towards a Tiger Moth. I said, with some amazement, "Who is that and what is he going to do?" I was told he was Arthur George, a local motor trader, who was seventy that day and was going to celebrate by a flight in the Moth. Mr George was helped into the machine by the engineer who swung the propeller, causing the engine to burst into life. The veteran taxied out, turned into the wind and took off. As an RAF Instructor under thirty, I was used to training pilots of eighteen and nineteen, and an elderly gentleman pilot of seventy was out of my league. I told the club treasurer that I would like to see Mr George land before I took over the flying club!'

There was little cause for worry, Arthur George was a pioneer of civil aviation with a listing of No. 19 in the Royal Aero Club's Register of Pilots. A partner in the Newcastle motor company of George and Jobling, he learned his flying in the south east along with other well-known aviation pioneers like Lord Babrazon (the first man in the country to hold a pilot's licence).

J.D.'s arrival injected new life and purpose into Aero Club flying, though his tenure as Chief Flying Instructor was to be short-lived. After just one year, Newcastle Corporation offered him the post of Commandant of Newcastle Airport, which he accepted.

The early 1950s were difficult times for civil aviation and private flying. The country was still recovering from the traumatic effects of the Second World War; the population still suffered food rationing and clothes rationing; post-war Governments were in the throes of rebuilding industry and injecting new life-blood into the economy. Ex-servicemen were still pulling their civilian lives together and there was no great demand for air transport or civilian flying. Britain had not yet become air-minded. For example, travellers to the North American continent still crossed the Atlantic by ocean liner in the main.

In that difficult climate, James H. Denyer took up his new post as the chief executive of Newcastle Airport in 1952. Assessing the state of the airport in that year, he listed the following shortcomings:

> No airline, large or small, flew out of the airport.
> Equipment servicing the airport was out-dated.
> Back-up services were strictly limited.
> A proper security service was absent.
> The total staff numbered fourteen.
> Apart from a 200-yard 'acceleration strip' there was no runway.
> There was no fixed flare-path.
> Radar equipment for air traffic control was absent.
> Airport terminal and offices were located in wooden huts.
> Woolsington was 'unknown' to many northern businessmen and industrialists.

There was limited private flying and charter work at Newcastle, but that was all. Prior to the appointment of J.D., the airport was run by Dave Davico, an experienced former RAF Instructor and Eileen O'Kane, a first-class administrator (who was to become Assistant Director of Woolsington before her sudden death). They reported directly to the City Engineer, representing Newcastle Corporation. Following reorganisation, Davico moved across to the Aero Club to become Flying Instructor. Forty years ago, airport traffic control was in the hands of three women operating direction-finding radio sets and ground-to-air intercom. They were Margaret Horne (first woman ATC to be licensed), Jean Sharpe and Nina Graham.

There were so few permanent staff at Woolsington that employees had to be jacks-of-all-trades, and that included the Airport Commandant. As Jim recalled: 'We guided aircraft down, carried passengers' luggage, refuelled the aircraft and even manned the one fire tender. Those were hectic but exciting days. In the 'terminal', which consisted of only a few huts, was a little buffet where passengers could buy biscuits, tea or coffee. One day I received a complaint from the tea-lady that her spoons kept disappearing and she was down to her last one. I suggested, in jest, that she tie it to the counter. When I next called at the buffet bar, there was the spoon on a piece of string attached to a nail on the counter!'

To say that the airport was under-equipped and run down was putting it mildly. The floor of the 'terminal building' was covered in lino which had seen better days: 'I used to joke that I could gauge the wind speed by noting how far the lino lifted from the floor!'

The heating in the 'terminal' was very primitive. All heat was supplied by a coke stove situated in the centre of the hut complete with chimney pipe spiralling through the roof. It was the job of George 'Geordie' Wilkes to stoke up the stove early every morning. One of the first letters of complaint from a passenger to the new Commandant was from a businessman booked on the first flight of the day who had checked in early on a bitter winter's morning. He made a bee-line for the coke stove and planted his backside firmly on the top. Inside, the stove was burning nicely and the fierce heat singed his trousers!

Jim's cheeks and eyes crinkled with mirth as he recalled some of the antics they got up to in the very early days. If there was a long flight delay and passengers had to be victualled, 'Operation March' was introduced. The airline staff lined up the passengers in threes and marched them a fair distance to the airport restaurant (now the Aero Club) for a hot meal.

In the early 1950s, Jim was unhappy about the close proximity of the maintenance hangar to the 'terminal building'. On boarding an aircraft at the start of a flight, the thing a passenger least wanted see was an aircraft under maintenance without a propeller.

In those days the top priority was to persuade an airline to inaugurate services from Woolsington. When at last J.D. found an airline that was interested he had virtually to put his job on the line to keep them there.

Hunting Air Transport was the first airline to set up at Newcastle under the new Airport Commandant and begin scheduled services, employing the twin-engine Dakota. They joined a company called BKS which was operating charter services and short-haul holiday routes.

After two years of operations, Hunting decided to modernise their fleet, introducing the much-acclaimed turbo-prop Viscount airliner—but there was a qualification. The airport authority would have to spend money raising one section of grassy runway to the same permanent standard as the rest. When the runway improvement plan came before the municipal authority it became lost in red tape. Hunting then applied pressure, informing J.D. that unless the runway improvement was carried out immediately, they would leave Newcastle. That was the last thing in the world that the fledgling airport wanted.

Jim decided to take the bull by the horns, and persuaded the City Engineer to begin the work; although the Airport Committee knew what was going on, the improvement had not been submitted to the full Newcastle City Council. After the work was completed, J.D. was questioned at a City Council meeting about 'unauthorised' development at the airport. By that time, Hunting had announced that it would stay at Woolsington, and the stylish Viscount was flying out of Newcastle to popular acclaim, stemming any further criticism. Newcastle passengers could now fly in modern aircraft to destinations like Belfast, Amsterdam and Düsseldorf as well as London, all on schedule services.

The Airport Commandant's next priority was to find the money to install a modern flare path system. When he arrived in 1952, the procedure for illuminating the grass runway was almost Dickensian—it was the era of the 'goose-neck' flares. The procedure for illuminating the runway was for the ground crew to prepare the goose-necks, which were in fact a series of metal kettles filled with paraffin with large wicks sticking out of the kettle neck. They were placed every 100 feet on the runway and then ignited by the crew. It was an operation not without danger; all the flares had to be placed carefully down-wind before ignition to prevent the possibility of catching fire. After some time, the Commandant substituted glim-lamps. Although primitive by today's standards, the lamps were a great improvement on the old goose-necks which were held in reserve.

In order to carry out this new operation, ground crew would transport a large drum containing a roll of electric cable to the runway side. To every 100 foot of cable was attached a small glim-lamp, about the size of a car headlamp bulb, the whole being run alongside the runway. Once laid, the runway could be lit up at the flick of a switch. As Jim Denyer put it 'That was the hope—when the system lit up, a cheer went up from the ground crew.' After the close of night operations, the crew would rewind the cable and return the drum to store until required again.

Eventually, a modern flare-path system was installed featuring underground electric cable.

Another urgent priority at Woolsington was the need for radar RDF (Radio Direction Finding) equipment to improve air traffic control. Although eventually renamed, radar was invented by a Scot, Sir Watson-Watt, in the early 1930s, and was long since seen as a breakthrough for aircraft identification and control at night or in fog. Newcastle had none.

It was a 'red letter day' for Newcastle Airport when the airport manager persuaded the Corporation to purchase a set in 1954. In placing the order for the latest Decca 424 Radar, Newcastle proved to be in the vanguard as no one else had it. Though the Royal Air Force had placed a vast order with Decca, set Mark 1, No. 1, was installed first at Woolsington where it had to win approval from the Service. The 424 system was installed by Decca technical staff based on Tyneside who maintained marine radar. That had the added advantage of drawing on spares and servicing locally, which meant that the equipment was rarely out of service. Following installation, J.D rushed off to do a quick course on the operation of the set and initially was the only one qualified as an operator: 'There were times when I had to drop what I was doing and run to the control tower to help bring in an aircraft in difficulty,' he recalled. Eventually several controllers were trained to operate the equipment.

The Decca Radar proved to be a valuable electronic life-line for aircraft in bad weather. Soon after it was installed it dealt with one air-borne emergency which helped to save more than thirty lives. The Airport Commandant could recall this drama of the fifties as though it were yesterday.

'In the summer of 1956 Captain Jack Jessop took off from Woolsington flying a twin-engine Dakota (DC-3) with a full load of passengers bound for Jersey. They were leaving shocking weather at home for the summer sun of the Channel Islands. As the Dakota lifted off from Woolsington, the pilot was confronted with a cloud base of 300 feet and visibility of less than 1,000 metres.'

The flight of the DC-3 was not destined to arrive in the sunny Channel Isles. The aircraft was approaching Darlington when there was a 'horrible bang' from the wing of the Dakota which told the crew that one of their engines had packed up. Captain Jessop and First Officer Jock Rennie decided that the best plan was to turn about and head back to base. They had only been flying their new course for a few minutes when a new emergency developed—a fire-warning light appeared on the one good engine. This was now a most critical condition with the chance that the aircraft might go out of control.

When this information was radioed back to Woolsington, the air traffic controller, Alan Jerams, who had picked up the Dakota on his radar tube, quickly summoned the Commandant to the control tower.

Jim Denyer recalls: 'Captain Jessop was flying through thick cloud with zero visibility as I operated a stepped down approach to Woolsington of 300 feet per mile. By radio and radar link we kept the aircraft on centre-line approach, giving ranges at regular intervals. First Officer Rennie had his eyes glued to the cockpit window to catch the first break in the clouds.

'Because of the atrocious weather conditions and the state of the aircraft we knew that we had only one chance of bringing the machines and its passengers into Woolsington safely.

'The seconds ticked by and as the radar screen showed the plane almost over the airport it suddenly popped out of the clouds with the runway becoming visible to the pilot. The landing had still to be made, and with a drastic reduction of engine power to cope with a full load of passengers and luggage.

'Jessop made a shallow turn and coming into the approach had to thump the Dakota down at speed, swinging it to the left and braking to pull up in the grass. A disaster that might have taken place didn't, thanks to the expertise of the Dakota crew and radar control at base.'

Forty years ago at a small airport with limited facilities and services, the Airport Commandant and every member of staff had to be prepared to act in an emergency. A fire-fighting emergency was a good example. If an aircraft in serious trouble was approaching Woolsington a bell would sound in the control tower, as a result of which staff would drop everything and run to help man the fire engines. After the emergency had been dealt with, staff would resume their normal duties. At Newcastle in 1952 there was one two-wheel-drive 200 gallon fire engine and two ex-local authority fire brigade staff. Other airport staff picked up fire fighting expertise by on-the-job training.

One emergency related to a fire under the wooden terminal building. J.D. was one of the first to tackle the trouble, and he and another staff member moved so quickly that a serious blaze was averted.

In those early days, the onslaught of a severe winter played havoc with the operation of the airport. The primitive snow-clearing equipment consisted of two small snow ploughs pushed by farm tractors, backed up by the entire airport staff wielding shovels! Heavy snow falls, freezing temperatures coupled with high winds, created heart-break situations for the tiny band of workers fighting to keep the airfield open.

J.D. recalls: 'We tried our damnedest to beat the elements but you could not really win. Our bad weather plan was to try and clear a taxi-way and runway path to allow aircraft to land. It was imperative to avoid banks of snow building up at the runway edges because of the clearance needed by aeroplane propellers. 'The cross wind was the worst. It would swing aircraft round on snowy, icy surfaces which could be a frightening business. Sometimes, after a very heavy fall of snow, we could not drive up the access road to the airport, and often I have walked to work in bad winters. Unfortunately, some air travellers did not understand the demand that snow-clearing imposed on the staff. Clearing an airport of snow to allow the movement of aircraft is a much more complex business than clearing roads.

'I recall one freezing February morning in the 1970s, following twenty-four hours of heavy snowfall—and a constant battle to keep the airport open—a number of businessmen arrived to fly to London. They complained about the state of the airport roads which had not had much attention, resulting in them having to walk through snow from their cars to the terminal.

'I explained that the first priority was to clear runway and taxi-way to enable aircraft to operate, which had been done. There was little point in clearing access roads if planes could not fly out (nobody could argue with that). Being sensible gentlemen they understood and were only too happy to board the flight for Heathrow!'

One businessman once told the airport manager he would do better with snow clearing if he treated the runway areas with salt and sand like the Corporation did the roads. Mr Denyer pointed out the high corrosive factor of salt and the damage it would do to the structure and moving parts of an aeroplane. 'The man gave me a sickly grin when he realised the folly of his remark,' recalls Jim. Even today, with modern snow ploughs and equipment, clearing an airport like Newcastle after heavy snow is a mammoth exercise. For example, removing the volume of snow from Woolsington after a very heavy fall is the equivalent of clearing the A696 of snow from Ponteland to Otterburn, a matter of some twenty miles.

Running Newcastle Airport in the early days presented many challenges; one of them was to try and make North East business and industry air-minded. During the 1950s the airport manager was out and about two or three times per week speaking to various organisations about the advantages of air travel and how it contributed to the future prosperity of the region.

There were a few local industrialists like Sir John Hunter, of Swan Hunter and Wigham Richardson and Sir Claude Gibb of C.A. Parsons who were pushing Newcastle Corporation to carry out improvements to the airport. At that time the airport was run by a single authority, Newcastle, who were confronted by the huge finance necessary to build a new airport and terminal. Only the combined forces of several local authorities could take on that kind of financial burden. Aware of the need to modernise was Col. Robert Mould-Graham, chairman of the Newcastle Airport Committee who recognised the time had arrived to put Newcastle on the aviation map.

As a result, in 1955 John Atkinson, Newcastle's Town Clerk, wrote to many North East local authorities asking them to join Newcastle in producing a development plan to build a modern airport.

'The response was lukewarm. The benefit to the region that would result from such a project, which would attract prestige airlines, had not sunk in,' J.D. recalls

It seems almost bizarre today to look back and retell some of the 'cloak and dagger' operations that were dreamt up to 'hide' the real Woolsington from important businessmen flying in from Europe and other foreign centres.

One devious operation was linked to a forthcoming visit to Newcastle by a group of German industrialists with whom John Hunter, the ship builder and ship-repairer, was eager to land a large contract. He was embarrassed at the thought of high-powered Germans leaving a modern airport and arriving at Woolsington to be confronted by a little grassy strip and a collection of old wooden huts. When he came to see the airport manager about the visit, he asked if anything could be done to 'hide' the airport terminal hut from the visiting Germans. Jim came up with an idea that would have done credit to a war-time special operations exercise.

He explained his 'decoy' plan to John Hunter: two Rolls Royce chauffeur-driven limousines would draw up to the door of the aircraft on the side of the aircraft facing away from the terminal hut. That would be achieved by arranging for the aircraft to enter the apron via the taxi-way, coming to rest with the  plane's exit door facing the airfield side. As soon as the Germans had de-planed they would be directed into the waiting cars and driven away at speed via the apron onto the main highway leading into the city.'

On the day of the visit the Elizabethan arrived on schedule and everything worked to plan. At the end of the day, the band of foreign industrialists had been impressed by Tyne ship-building and were happy to sign contracts. There was a small hiccup. As the visitors arrived back at Woolsington for the return flight and saw the primitive airfield they threw up their hands and declared in one voice: 'This is not where we landed!'

That was the kind of manoeuvre that Jim Denyer had to get up to in the early days to protect the image of the North East region !

Both John Hunter and Claude Gibb saw the development of a modern airport as not just a matter of prestige for the region, but a valuable means of attracting inward investment. C.A. Parsons was one of the first Tyneside companies to fly their own aircraft out of Woolsington, servicing it from their own hangar.

# THE MYSTERY PLANE OF WOOLSINGTON

Some of the stories that came out of Newcastle Airport in the 1950s were so filled with intrigue, they could have come straight out of a Frederick Forsyth best seller. One such story centres on the amazing saga of 'The Mystery Plane of Woolsington'.

The saga began one day in the late 1950s when a four-engined DC-4 Canadair arrived over Newcastle Airport and asked permission to land. After landing the large plane, the crew checked into traffic control, gave the name and address of the owner and disappeared into thin air, not to be seen again. When the airport manager sent demands for landing and parking fees to the owner there was no response. Extensive inquiries were then launched by Woolsington but no intelligence could be gathered. The Canadair just stood on the tarmac at Newcastle, chocked up and surrounded by mystery.

As the weeks turned into months with no news of the owner, Mr Denyer decided that the plane should be moved from the valuable space on the tarmac onto grass, where the aircraft wheels were planked to prevent it sinking into the ground. After a considerable time Jim decided to bring matters to a head. More than £1,000 was owed in parking and other fees so the strange aircraft, which appeared to be in good flying order,would have to go.

After taking legal advice and applying to the appropriate authority it was decided to hold a public auction of the Canadair at Woolsington. Advertisements were placed in the aeronautical and the local Press. The story of the mystery plane for sale created much public interest and when the day of the auction arrived members of the public stood alongside specialised dealers. To the surprise of most people, the reaction from the bidders was only lukewarm.

Bidding for the four-engined aircraft opened at £800 and stuck at £1,200 at which point a Newcastle night-club owner decided that this was a bargain too good to miss!

Having bought the plane, Mr Abe Levy, one of the Levy brothers who owned the then internationally known 'Dolce Vita' night club in Newcastle, considered what might be done with it. One scheme was to strip out the airliner seats and convert the plane into a restaurant and club, located at the airport. This idea failed to get off the ground, so the Levy brothers then sold the aircraft to a buyer from down south for more money than they paid for it! All in all, the Canadair experience had not been a bad one for the Levys—they were in pocket and their night-club had received hundreds of pounds worth of free publicity.

The story of the Canadair was far from finished. Some time later, the telephone rang on the airport manager's desk to inform him that three gum-chewing Americans had arrived and were asking to see him. Dressed in leather flying jackets and looking like barn-storming aviators from the American past, they produced papers authorising them to fly out the Canadair. By this time staff at the airport were getting very suspicious about the background to this mystery plane. HM Customs Officers held up the departure of the plane for three days while they made extensive inquiries.The Canadair carried a Canadian Air Force serial number, but no British registration number as required by aviation law. It was then that the American flight engineer came out with the strangest request that Jim Denyer had heard in a life-time of aviation.

He wanted to know where he could obtain washable white paint! Let J.D. continue the story: 'I asked him why he wanted it. He came straight out with the reason. He wanted to paint the new registration number on the aircraft with paint that would wash off when they flew though cloud so that when the plane landed at Amsterdam it would carry only its old service number, cloaking its identity. I sent the American to see the BKS engineer, Nick Carter, who very quickly told him where to go!'

Eventually the Canadair was cleared to leave for Amsterdam and Jim discovered later that on arriving there, the crew was met by an armed guard and arrested in connection with illegal cargo-carrying. Nevertheless, the aircraft managed to fly out of Amsterdam and went back to its shady business, thought to be gun-running.

The last J.D. heard of the 'Woolsington Mystery Plane' was that it had crashed and broken its back on a remote African air strip—and as it crashed guns and ammunition spewed out of its belly. That was a sad end to a beautiful aeroplane.

Back at Woolsington there were many problems demanding attention. One centred on the parlous state of flying operations at the Newcastle Aero Club. As J.D. recalls: 'The club was in financial difficulties and could probably have lasted out a couple more years before folding up, which I was loathe to see. I persuaded Newcastle Corporation to take the flying side of the club over, as a result of which I became manager of the first Municipal Flying School in the country.' He remembered that in those days, the school owned Tiger Moths and Austers. Tuition charges were reasonably high: £3 5s. per hour dual instruction and £2 10s. solo. (In an economic job market then, £10 per week was a good average wage). The school was fortunate to be served by a dedicated staff. Flying Instructor Dave Davico (an ex-RAF Instructor) was assisted by Freddie Bayne and Bill Baines. Alan Irwin was Chief Engineer assisted by Bob Forsyth, Alec Imrie and Joe Turner. Any commercial work undertaken, including aerial photography was flown by J.D. with photographers Roy Gibson or Alan Harrison. J.D. also carried out flying licence tests.

When Jim Denyer and his assistant, Eileen O'Kane took over the running of the flying school, they virtually doubled their work load. In spring and summer, during day-light hours they closed the airport office at 5 p.m., crossed over to the flying school and started work there. J.D. taught and flew pupils until dusk while Eileen took the payments and kept the books: 'We used to joke about it and say that we worked thirty-six hours a day, eight days a week!' Weekend working was the norm. It was hard but that sort of dedication was needed to develop the airport and the Aero Club initially. In the first year or two under new management the flying school continued to lose money, resulting in some 'hard bargaining' sessions with the City Treasurer who reminded J.D. that he was using rate-payers' money. By the mid-fifties the school was breaking even and then began to pay its way. By 1960, when the Aero Club was restored to full financial health, it again resumed responsibility for running the flying school.

The first light at the end of the tunnel for Newcastle took place in the mid 1950s when London began to take notice of the operations of the Newcastle Flying School. Out of the blue, J.H. Denyer was invited to the Royal Aero Club annual dinner where he was presented with the Lennox-Boyd Trophy by the Government Aviation Minister of the day.

This prestigious award was given to Newcastle to mark the efficient manner in which the operation was run. Sharing the honour with Jim Denyer was Dave Davico, the Chief Flying Instructor.

Although there was a long road ahead before Woolsington established itself firmly on the aviation map of Great Britain, things were on the move and within the next decade a fine, modern terminal would be erected.

# Chapter III

## LIFE IN THE RAF

## ADVENTURES IN WAR AND PEACE

For thousands of young men leaving their jobs in 1939 and 1940 to serve their country at war, there was a special attraction about joining the Royal Air Force. By the end of the first year of war, the RAF had already proved itself as a crack fighting service, particularly for its outstanding feats during the Battle of Britain.

To put on the RAF blue uniform for the first time was a proud moment for the future air crews. James Henry Denyer was no exception when his call-up papers arrived at the age of seventeen. He reported to Air Crew Assembly point in North London after which he was dispatched to the Initial Training Wing. He soon received a minor shock: he discovered that in early training days in the RAF there was plenty of marching—the very thing he had hoped to avoid by joining the Air Force!

After weeks of foot-slogging, young Jim Denyer was posted to RAF Station Woodley, a former flying club airfield near Reading to commence flying training which went well. He soon discovered that he had a natural aptitude for flying, a gift that took him to his first solo flight without any real problems. The memory of that first solo remained vivid: 'I flew a Miles Magister, went through the regulation drills and manoeuvres, and, coming in to land, I felt so proud that I did not appreciate that the instructor was not sitting in the cockpit behind me! It was an experience that I shall never forget.'

By the end of 1940 the 'Boys in Blue' had become figures of popular acclaim, their feats plastered all over the national Press. That prompted a certain amount of bantering from members of the other Services who sometimes taunted airmen with the cry: 'The Glamour Boys' and 'Brylcreem Boys'.

Those taunts did not trouble Jim, who after passing through part one of flying training, received orders to sail to Canada for onward posting to the USA for extended flying training. His arrival in America opened up new horizons for an airman in his late teens both in aviation and a new way of life. His first surprise on arriving at a Flying Training School in the deep South was to discover that the RAF boys would undergo the American West Point system of training, one of strict discipline and regulations tied to an honour system. That system assumed that a cadet would always tell the truth, and in extreme cases would report himself for any breach of regulations. A cadet reporting himself to an officer or upper classman would receive demerit points, depending on the gravity of the offence. Five points (known as 'gigs') meant one hour's marching with full pack during the cadet's weekend leave. Needless to say, British cadets on the receiving end of five 'gigs' took a dim view of marching up and down in front of HQ while pretty girlfriends were waiting for them in their large 'limos' beyond the barrier at the guard-room.

Away from the training camp, the American deep South in the 1940s remained a racist society; segregation was the order of the day; privileged whites lauded it over the blacks. Jim Denyer experienced a taste of the racist society when he and his pals took off on an off duty trip to Americas the nearest small town to the camp. Entering a bar, they had hardly sipped their drinks when a Police car arrived, ushered them out and escorted them to the local Police Station.

There the RAF men were lectured by the Police Chief about the protocol of segregation. 'That bar is for niggers, keep away,' he told them. Whites had their own bars, restaurants and buses; a negro had to step off the pavement to allow a white person to pass. Jim recalls 'it was like pre-Civil War times, we in the RAF could hardly comprehend it. Relationships have certainly changed since the 1940s.'

Racism apart he found life in war-time America convivial enough. Compared to belt-tightening Britain at war, this was the land of plenty. No shortages of any kind; vast quantities of food; and a friendly society graced by a nation of attractive girls led by the glamourous Southern Belles. At the same time, family life in the South was close-knit and regulated in the white communities. Often to the chagrin of love-starved young British pilots, the family code provided for the presence of chaperons for their daughters! Jim loved the American families and their way of life, just the same. Every RAF airman was befriended and entertained in American homes. He remembered: 'I still have the front door key to the home of the Hilliers, of Fort Valley, Georgia who welcomed and adopted me all those years ago.'

During his flying training, he was posted to several US flying schools piloting aircraft like the Stearman, the Vultee and the Harvard. He saw at first hand the high proficiency of the American pilot, certainly equal to his British counterpart. After successfully completing his flying training he had the experience of being awarded two sets of wings: RAF Wings presented by a Group Captain and the metallic USAAF wings presented by an American Army Air Force Colonel.

Returning to the UK, Jim found himself at RAF Little Rissington for a conversion course to twin-engine aircraft. He was then transferred to RAF Ouston as a staff pilot at the night-fighter navigators' Operational Training Unit.

That posting to Ouston in Northumberland in 1943 was to open up a new and far-reaching chapter for Sgt.-Pilot Denyer—a series of events would unfold that would radically change his life

At this period of World War II, RAF Station Ouston was one of the leading airfields in the North of England. As a fighter station it employed first Hurricanes and then Spitfires for the defence of the North, while also operating an OTU. In addition, for one period, Beaufighters and Defiants flew out of Ouston on night-fighter patrols.

In many ways, Ouston, set in wild moorland twelve miles to the west of Newcastle, was an unlikely site to set up a new airfield. It was really no surprise that when the Air Ministry designated the site in 1938, local authority officials received the news with incredulity.

RAF Ouston, nevertheless, went on to establish itself as a leading war-time station in the north. It was while he was stationed at Ouston that J.D. met the engaging character and Australian flier called Keith Miller. Looking back, J.D. chuckles over the story of Miller and the cricket team at RAF Ouston.

Any cricket follower who watched test match cricket in the post-war years, and the great clashes between England and Australia will tell you that Miller was one of the finest all-rounders to play test cricket for Australia. During the war years, he was not so well-known, though before coming to the UK to train as a pilot he had already become a member of the Victoria State Team as a batsman.

J.D.'s amusing tale centres on the day that RAF Station Ouston decided to form their own cricket team. Miller, like other sporting personnel at the station, added his name to the mess list asking for interested parties. When the team was picked for the inaugural match, Miller discovered that he was chosen as twelfth man and ended up as scorer. Later, when the Ouston selectors picked their team for their second match, Miller was included. A somewhat startled body of selectors were informed that he was sorry but he was unavailable. He had been chosen to play for Australia against England at Lords!

As J.D. put it: 'There must have been a few red faces among the selectors at Ouston, particularly as Miller scored a century for his country.' It was typical of the man that he bore no ill-will and was happy to turn out for the Station team in their subsequent matches. Cricket lovers will recall the classic fast bowling attack for Australia in post-war test matches of Ray Lindwall and Keith Miller. Miller, the crowd favourite and instinctive cavalier, could be just as brilliant and devastating with the bat. Some people say it was not surprising that Miller became a fighter-pilot with the Australian Air Force—he was named Keith Ross Miller after the early aviators, Keith and Ross Smith.

A host of other characters flying from RAF Ouston in those war-time years included Michael O'Leary, a much decorated navigator (later an instructor) who was affectionately known as the 'Mad Irishman.' One of his escapades was to jump into the driver's cab of an electric tram and drive it up Westgate Road in Newcastle when he missed his last transport back to base. 'The spirit of living for the day was captured by that band of well-decorated and tour-expired navigators flying out of Ouston,' remembers J.D. 'They were all great guys, hail-fellow-well-met, who enjoyed a party when flying was done.'

Loath to leave the North East, Jim next found himself posted to RAF Spitalgate near Grantham where he flew Blenheims, a well-known early night-fighter of the war. After Grantham, he continued his flying career at RAF Charterhall in Scotland.

Charterhall was a busy station; as well as fulfilling a role for fighter operations it also was a base for the training of pilots to fly the Beaufighter, a favourite night-fighting machine among RAF pilots. However, accidents were not uncommon at Charterhall which acquired the nick-name, 'Slaughterhall' among aircrew. Another training machine used there was the Beaufort.

Flt. Sgt.-Pilot Jim Denyer liked the Beaufighter, particularly the Mark VI machine. 'It was a large, heavy powerful metal aeroplane with twin Hercules engines armed with eight Browning machine guns and I loved it,' he said.

It was while flying a Beaufort with a Polish W/O Pilot/Instructor that Jim came close to meeting his maker. When one of the twin engines of the aircraft failed over the sea, J.D. turned the plane for home. On receiving clearance to land during final approach he was staggered to hear that another aircraft had received clearance to line up and take off on the same runway. It was obvious that it would not have cleared the runway by the time Jim's machine crossed the threshold, so there was no choice but to open the throttle on the good engine to overshoot and execute another circuit.

Jim picks up the story: 'half way round we knew we were not going to make it, the only course open was to turn across the active runway and make a crash landing with wheels up.' This meant our approach would be made across the Beaufighter dispersal where a pilot was in the act of strapping himself in and unaware of us. The ground crew, aware of the danger, dived to the ground, we missed them by twenty feet and then we reared towards the control tower. We thumped down on the grass, though under control, and the force of the impact (helped by my navigator bracing his feet on the back of my seat) caused the cockpit seat to break away, throwing me violently forward. I was saved from being thrown into the plane's gunnery well and chewed up by the aircraft's under-belly only by the control column braking my slide.'

After it was all over, Jim looked at the damaged plane and reckoned that he and his colleague had been lucky though the Polish pilot had been knocked unconscious during the emergency landing, hitting his head on a gun sight. Jim had a long look at the under-belly of the Beaufort which had been torn away. That was just one of the traumatic experiences of Jim's war-time career, though 'Lucky Jim' came through them all without serious injury.

After Charterhall, he was posted to RAF Winfield where for the first time he flew the 'wonder aircraft' of the war, the beautifully proportioned, all wood Mosquito, faster and more manoeuvrable than the Beaufighter. From there he joined the prestigious No. 29 Squadron, flying Mosquitos on operations from the North London RAF airfield of Hunsdon.

The Mosquito was equipped with one of the best kept secrets of the war, known simply as 'AI'. This small air interception radar set enabled RAF navigators to pick up hostile aircraft at night and attack them. Jim's navigator was Viv Kellard who became a close friend. To be successful with the AI only a combination of both pilot and navigation skills would do. The job of the navigator radar operator, watching his electronic 'tube', was to get his pilot within visual range of the enemy, after which J.D. could go in for the kill after first identifying the target aircraft.

The Denyer-Kellard team were soon in action carrying out what the RAF called 'Intruder Operations'. The role of the Mosquitos was to patrol enemy fighter airfields during Allied bomber raids, and shoot down anything that tried to take off. It sounds straightforward enough, but these hazardous missions were testing in the extreme.

First, in order not to reveal to the Luftwaffe that a bombing raid was imminent, the Mosquito Squadron had to fly at very low level to get under enemy radar and escape detection. One gets some idea of the challenge if one knows that these raids were made at night over strange territory. An imperative was for pilot and navigator to study maps of the aircraft's course, and mark heights that gave them a safety margin at low level. The height indicator, a radio altimeter, in the cockpit was a good aid but had no capacity to forecast land contours not yet reached.

It was almost a relief to arrive safe and on time over an enemy airfield, though phase two of the operation was just as demanding as the 'roof top' flying to get them there. The mode was to pick out and fly a patrol line around the airfield for something approaching an hour. If German fighters took off you endeavoured to shoot them down.

The skills of any pilot were tested by the demand to stay on the patrol line in the dark, particularly if there were no visual markers to fly between, and allowing for wind-drift. After completing this phase and after the RAF bombers had done their work, other Mosquitos would remain over the target airfield to catch returning enemy fighters.

J.D. summed it up this way: 'The Mosquito crews were stimulated by the challenge of intruder operations—the Luftwaffe held every advantage, radar protection, anti-aircraft guns and friendly airfields close at hand.'

A different kind of operation was known as 'Day Ranger'—a search and destroy mission in which Mosquitos flew out in the early hours to arrive over German airfields at dawn, proceeding to shoot up any enemy aircraft dispersed on the ground. If the Mosquitos circled for a second attack, that could invite real danger. By that time the German ack-ack batteries had woken up and unleased a fierce barrage at the British fliers. It was not unusual on missions like this to be hit by pieces of flak.

On all missions against the enemy, the AI radar set was a key factor in locating hostile aircraft. It was such a well kept secret that RAF Intelligence and the British propaganda machine fed misinformation to the Press about the reasons for the success of their night-fighters. In fact a legend was born after a brilliant pilot, John Cunningham, started to knock German aircraft out of the sky with some regularity. In order to hoodwink the Germans, the Press was informed that Cunningham had extraordinary night vision which enabled him to see in the dark like a cat. Lapping up the story, Fleet Street coined a nickname for him—'Cat's Eyes Cunningham'. It was true that he became an ace night-fighter pilot, though by nature a modest and tolerant man who used to cringe each time he read his sobriquet in the newspapers. 'Group Captain Cunningham, who shot down twenty German aircraft was a brilliant pilot who never panicked' recalled J.D. Jim pointed out that Cunningham's success was linked to the expertise of his navigator/radar operator Jimmie Rawnsley, an engineer by profession who was one of the pioneers of air radar navigation. 'The night fighter crew had to gel together to succeed' was how J.D. put it.

The Cunningham-Rawnsley partnership was the perfect combination, an excellent pilot and outstanding AI operator, making one of the war's top night-fighting teams.

J.D. ran into Cunningham after the war when he was chief test pilot for the de Havilland Aircraft Company, helping to pioneer the development of the first British jet passenger aircraft, the beautiful Comet. When the talk turned to war-time days, J.D. was somewhat surprised to be told by Cunningham that his eyesight was no better than the average! Cunningham, who successfully tested the Comet into service was much decorated during the war, receiving the DSO with two Bars, the OBE, and the DFC with Bar.

Another legend, at first created around Cunningham and then exploited by the Ministry of Food to persuade war-time Britons to eat more vegetables, was the 'magic' quality of the carrot in the diet. It was put about that Cunningham's 'superhuman sight' was nourished by a diet of carrots, aiding his night-vision. While that was an exaggeration, it is a fact that the vitamins found in carrots can be a contributory factor to eye health. According to Jim, even with the benefit of 'AI' fitted in the plane, it helped a pilot to be able to see as much as possible in the dark. It was common practice before boarding an aircraft during night missions for pilots to sit around with red-lensed goggles on. Exposure to artificial light could affect the 'visual purple' (night vision) of the eye.

Among the many RAF Stations he flew into during the war, one Jim Denyer is unlikely to forget is Milfield, situated five miles North of Wooler. This was a top Fighter Leader School which specialised in teaching low-level attack, playing an important role in making the RAF the supreme attackers.

Milfield-trained pilots played a significant role in the D-Day invasion, and the tradition has continued right up to the Gulf War when RAF pilots were the only Allied Force which could invade and bomb Iraqi aerodromes at very low level. The techniques of strafing, dive-bombing and rocket firing were taught to a high degree of proficiency at Milfield—using live ammunition. British, Commonwealth and American pilots arrived at Milfield during the war to train on Typhoons, Spitfires and Hurricanes. As Jim recalls those days: 'We did much low-level flying around north Northumberland and southern Scotland. We flew so low the pilots christened the runs "sheep shearing".' The roar of aircraft engines at low-level was intensely annoying to Northumberland farmers and their cattle, but it was war-time. Of course, low-level training continued in peace-time when the grumbles from the farmers were much more vocal, though since Tornados blazed a trail in the Gulf War, criticism has been rather more muted.

In the last year of the war, Jim Denyer and Viv Kellard flew together in first of all, Beaufighters, and then Mosquitos. Both fliers were to finish the war unscathed though sadly, after Kellard had left the Service and joined Air India as a pilot, he contracted cerebral malaria and died in the Far East.

When J.D. first arrived at No. 29 Squadron he met a mission-hardened navigator called Alan Taylor from Whitley Bay; Taylor and his Mosquito pilot had numerous victories over German aircraft in different theatres of war. Since the last war, Denyer and Taylor have kept in touch with one another through the years, and Taylor was a guest of honour at Jim's farewell dinner to mark his retirement after nearly forty years service to Newcastle Airport.

Many books have already been written about the heroic fighter pilots of the Battle of Britain, and the outstanding RAF pilots from all branches of the Service. But J.D. had to wait until he was running Newcastle Airport to meet two of the biggest names of the air war of World War II—Johnnie Johnson and Douglas Bader. When Newcastle built its first modern air terminal in 1967 and the Aero Club moved to the premises it occupies today, the club was re-opened by Johnson who was elected a vice-president, a post he still retains.

Although J.D. never flew with Douglas Bader, as a fellow pilot he never ceased to be impressed by his brilliant flying and shrewd tactical brain in the air which made him the scourge of the Luftwaffe. Bader, who lost his legs in a pre-war flying accident, epitomised the man of courage who overcame a devastating injury to serve his country. 'Bader was a legend' said J.D. 'Without doubt he was a great man and flier, an inspiration to other servicemen who lost limbs fighting in the last war.' He had few peers when it came to drawing up strategy and tactics of fighting in the air. It was Bader with Leigh-Mallory, Air Officer commanding 12 Group, who pioneered the 'Big Wing' echelons (initially opposed by Fighter Command) which concentrated fire power in numbers, much to the consternation of the Luftwaffe.

Looking back on his war-time flying career, one memory that remains is that of long, cramped hours spent in the Mosquito's small cockpit, particularly gruelling on long-distance missions. Only the technology of fitting 100 gallon drop tanks under the wings made those marathon missions possible. One such war-time mission was to Schlessenheim, near Lake Constance which, with an hour's patrol over target was more than six hours flying. On a flight of that duration, physical demands of nature assume special significance—the pilot of a Mosquito, strapped into the cockpit with the control column between his legs, was barely able to move. What would be a quick visit to the 'mobile loo' for bomber crews on long flights, became a minor ordeal for Mosquito pilots.

'To commune with nature you tried to lift yourself up off your seat and find the funnel into the urine bottle in low-level cockpit lighting. If the demand was much greater, you had it on your lap on the parachute seat and lived with that,' was how J.D. remembered it.

On those long flights there was little time to be bored. Flying over enemy territory demanded vigilance, German night-fighters could be up in a flash. Radio contact with accompanying aircraft had to he kept, the target course continually verified and up-dated. There was an additional risk of being on the receiving end of 'friendly fire'. A good example was the night J.D. and his navigator were returning from an extended mission when the Americans identified their aircraft as 'hostile' and put in an attack. J.D. tells it this way: 'We had just crossed the front line on the return journey and over France I heard from my radio an American ground controller vector an American Black Widow night-fighter on what I presumed to be a hostile target. It took a few seconds to sink in, but the course given was my course!

'I told my navigator, Viv Kellard, to check his rear view radar for contact and altered course 30 degrees to starboard. Within ten seconds, the ground controller gave his night-fighter the same alteration. Although we switched on our IFF (Identification, Friend or Foe) and identified as Friendly, there was no reaction from the ground.

'I said to Viv, we'll have some fun with this chap but keep an eye on his range which was five miles and closing. I opened throttles and increased speed, knowing full well that the Mosquito was the faster of the two aircraft. The Black Widow pilot increased his speed. I now thought it prudent to break off this engagement and inform the Americans who I was, which I did in no uncertain terms. The controller and pilot at once broke off and wished us a safe return. I shudder to think what might have happened if I had not been listening out on that radio frequency that night!'

The RAF crew's troubles were not entirely over; crossing over the Channel they ran into bad weather and encountered fog over their squadron base which necessitated a 'Fido' landing. 'Fido' was then the Fog Intensity Dispersal Operation which employed flaming paraffin flares to clear a path down the runway for landing. That was not the easiest of landings for a tired crew at the end of a long mission, the heat turbulence throwing the aircraft around at the critical stage of landing which was below fifty feet. The Mosquito landed safely. All that remained for this air crew before they could take a well-earned rest was to proceed through debriefing and eat a hot meal. Jim recalls that the solace of sleep sometimes evaded fighter pilots, despite their fatigue. In his own case, he was sometimes restless after completing operations, mentally re-flying the mission and thinking about what he should, or should not have done.

Although the world of medicine was studying the effect of stress and fatigue on the efficiency of war-time pilots, the pilots themselves were unaware of any physical or psychological complications. Sometimes, tour-expired RAF pilots experienced severe fatigue and even mental problems.

Jim Denyer said that he was so young at the time of the air war that he never had the chance of experiencing the problems suffered by the veterans of the air. 'The very young pilots like myself were ignorant of any physical or mental backlash from flying war planes; we just flew these very fast aeroplanes at low-level at night and got on with it.'

When World War II came to an end, he had to think seriously about his future. He knew that leaving the RAF would be a wrench; despite the horrors of war, he had taken a liking to life in the service. He enjoyed the special camaraderie common among crews of the RAF, and he found the business of piloting aeroplanes most rewarding. It was not surprising, therefore, that he elected to remain in the Air Force, once hostilities had ceased. His promotion from Warrant Officer Pilot to Pilot Officer in 1945, rewarding him with an Extended Service Commission was to reinforce his life in the RAF for the next six years, a period in which he was further promoted, attaining the rank of Flight Lieutenant by the late 1940s.

After fifty years of flying he still preferred flying through the night. 'It is something that gets into your blood, that stealthy business of clambering into a cockpit in the dark, knowing that soon you would be flying on instruments through the night sky. Flying above a large city illuminated by an electric carpet of twinkling lights can be a glorious sight for a pilot at night,' is how he explained it. 'Flying for me is more relaxing and peaceful at night, though it is vital to remain vigilant as it is easy to lose track of where you are and where you are going.' During his war-time missions, he always felt that it was more difficult for the enemy to locate and engage him in the darkness.

One little cameo of flying through the stars remained an indelible memory. 'I was flying east along the North African coast before dawn and looked in wonder at the monstrous, golden glowing orb emerging over the horizon; the sight below was an unforgettable backdrop, animals of different shapes and sizes stirring in the first dawn light...I have seen a few dawns come up in my time but that North African canvas was a unique experience.' Not that he had divine astral experiences, or awareness of heavenly bodies, as one or two of the American astronauts claim to have had. 'Though the first time I flew above 30,000 feet my Meteor jet appeared to squat in space; there was no sense of movement in a silent world,' he recalled.

After the war, flying in the peace-time Royal Air Force, he found himself posted to Parachute Training Schools, first to Ringway (Manchester) and later to Upper Heyford. There he flew servicemen undergoing parachute training and discovered that for some it could be a very risky business. From time to time, accidents occurred to both aircraft and personnel, although J.D. dropped thousands of parachutists on exercises without mishap. He did that by following the tried and tested technique for drops. 'I always flew the Dakota slowly with the power held back to minimise the slip-stream; at the moment of jump I put the aircraft nose down, forcing the tail of the machine up thus allowing parachutists to fall safely under it.'

RAF life in post-war Britain was working out well for this one-time sheet metal worker. He was happily married to Mary from Newcastle, the girl he met at a war-time Woolsington dance, and in 1946 was promoted to Flying Officer. He continued to advance his career in the Royal Air Force, and by the time of the Berlin airlift had been promoted again.

At the end of the giant airlift to Germany in May 1949 he was posted to Little Rissington Central Flying School, and from there to RAF Cottesmore to begin a new aspect of his career as a flying instructor. He was by this time a Flight Lieutenant. Piloting the dual-control Percival Prentice and the Harvard training machines, he discovered that teaching young men to fly could be a reward in itself.

This period of RAF flying was an enjoyable one for J.D. As he recalled: 'I loved this part of my career. It was very rewarding to teach a pupil, seeing his progression in handling a machine until the point of proficiency when he was able to fly solo for the first time.'

He continued as a Senior RAF Instructor right up to 1951 when fate stepped in and and drew him into a new career in civilian life, becoming the Chief Flying Instructor of Newcastle upon Tyne Aero Club. Before that he was to take part in the biggest air transport operation ever organised to offer a life-line to a German city under siege. The story of the Berlin airlift is told in the next chapter.

# Chapter IV

## AIR DRAMA OVER BERLIN

## FLYING OFFICER DENYER FLIES TO CITY UNDER SIEGE

## MERCY MISSION BY RAF

In a life-time in aviation, one of Jim Denyer's greatest challenges was flying in the famous Berlin airlift, taking food, fuel and other vital commodities to starving German citizens from June 1948 to May 1949, in a round-the-clock operation with hostile aircraft in waiting. 'It was a hairy and harrowing experience, flying in all weathers,' was how he described it.

This biggest-ever transportation by air was launched after Russia shocked the Allies by imposing a blockade on Berlin in 1948, in the aftermath of World War II. Until that time, the city had been divided into sectors, and jointly administered by Britain, America and France together with Russia. This attempt by Russia to seize the whole of Berlin was based on the premise (which turned out to be false) that not even the Allies could keep a city of over 2,000,000 people alive by air supply alone. The Soviet coup had left nothing to chance, blocking all road and rail routes into Berlin, as well as the waterways.

When the Royal Air Force was placed on a war footing in 1948, Flying Officer Denyer, serving with 38 Group Transport Command, was one of many service pilots ordered to fly vital supplies into Berlin, the city under siege. From a pilot's point of view, the Berlin run was to turn out to be a most risky series of operations. The only entry into the German city was down three narrow air corridors, from which Allied pilots strayed at their peril: patrolling the sides of the corridors were Russian Yak fighter aircraft, waiting to punish any RAF transports which wandered off course. What made the operations all the more arduous was the handicap of flying slow moving, heavily laden Dakotas. It was more than unsettling, recalls J.D., if you were buzzed and pounced on by these fast moving jet fighters. One Russian ploy was to fly alongside the air corridors into the face of oncoming RAF transport machines, whose pilots were often struggling to hold the Dakotas on course in adverse weather conditions. Sometimes, J.D. remembers, there were incidents involving flak (anti aircraft fire) put up by Russian batteries. (The Dakotas were also known as the DC-3).

The need for food, fuel and other supplies was so desperately needed by the people of Berlin, that Britain, France and America blanketed the sky with cargo planes filled to capacity, operating both day and night.

J.D. said that the Berlin airlift was sharply etched in his memory. 'The Allied Air Forces' technique was to fly streams of aircraft at different given heights. The most difficult course to fly was the middle stream; with the sky packed with aircraft above and below you there was little room for error. The RAF Transports, of which I was one, flew the middle stream continuously.' Even the most severe weather conditions did not halt the airlift. As it happened, the winter of 1948 to '49 was a bad one. Flying Officer Denyer, as he was then, remembered the challenge of flying through fog, frost and blizzard. 'Keep the aircraft flying' was the order of the day. Transport aircraft, with known minor faults were directed into the operations, so urgent was the need to keep the lift going.

Although the Dakotas were equipped with heating equipment, the pilots had to be extra alert during severe freezing conditions as ice built up on the aircraft wings. 'At the right moment I had to switch in the "boot de-icer" to try and get rid of the ice'. On the tail of the Dakota and the leading edges of both wings were rubber sleeves with an inflater. When the pilot pressed the 'boot button' the sleeve inflated and cracked the ice. (Ice forming on wings can threaten the stability of an aeroplane, interfering with the aerodynamic behaviour patterns). Ice on propellers was another problem facing pilots on the Berlin run; the de-icers would cause pieces of ice which had formed on the propeller to be catapulted away at great speed. 'I can recall ice also flying off the engines behind the cockpit and striking the fuselage with a crash!' said J.D. After making one flight into Berlin and successfully returning to the British base at Lübeck, Jim discovered that the side of his Dakota fuselage was bent in by flying ice. With aeroplane propellers turning over at some 2,000 revolutions per minute, flying ice presented a real danger.

British, American and Allied aircraft between them flew into Berlin many of the necessities of life, apart from food and fuel. Manifests included clothes, medicines, razor blades and candles, sanitary towels and hot-water bottles and even newsprint to feed the Berlin newspaper presses in their propaganda battle with the Russians. In the early stages of the airlift, J.D. recalls flying out spare aircraft parts to Wunsdorf in order to keep the big 'Yorks' flying.

One cargo which caused a special problem was salt. It seeped through tiny holes in sacks stacked inside the machines and penetrated the aircraft floors, corroding metal control surfaces. Later it was found more prudent to switch this cargo to the Sunderland Flying Boats whose controls were built into the roof of the machine. The Sunderlands operated in and out of the River Elbe.

J.D. did not forget his most hated cargo—coal. Sacks were awkward to stack in the DC-3 , which was designed as a passenger and not a cargo-carrying aircraft—and coal dust seeped into every nook and cranny of the machine. Then there was the cargo of flour, which also caused problems. Flour dust with coal dust created a grime which formed on the interior of the aircraft and was hard to remove. Years later, long after the end of the Berlin airlift, DC-3s which had taken part still had traces of coal and flour dust in their structure.

In order to transfer into Berlin the many thousands of tons of cargo being flown into Germany, bases were set up at Wunsdorf, Fassburg and Lübeck, landing grounds that Denyer got to know well. Landing at any of those three—in the centre of a continuous stream of scores of aircraft all fully loaded—was a supreme test of a pilot's skill.

The 'armada' of aircraft that flew into Berlin every day was only made possible by the skill and coolness of radar control teams directing the operation from the ground. The radar controllers, strategically situated on the approaches of the Berlin airfields performed a highly synchronised task, passing on pilots from one to another as the machines made for final approaches. So congested was the sky, and so small was the interval between continuous landings that if a pilot made a mistake he was forced to abort the mission and return to base.

J.D. had no doubt about the great challenge the airlift set pilots. 'Flying the Berlin airlift was more challenging than flying on operations in World War II, greater skill was called for over longer periods.'

RAF Transport Command pilots were flying two continuous missions into the besieged city, which resulted in many hours at the controls of a machine without a break. J.D. recalls that he would take off in his Dakota in daylight with a full load of cargo, fly nonstop missions taking him through the night into the following day when he would land exhausted. 'To say that it was wearing was an understatement.'

There were anxious discussions among air crews when Transport Group ordered their pilots to fly three nonstop missions into Berlin instead of two as an experiment. The order had to soon be rescinded. 'It had to be stopped as pilots were dropping off to sleep at the controls of their aircraft,' recalled J.D.

Sometimes the RAF planes went to the rescue of women, children and the elderly who were suffering from the effects of the siege in a bleak winter. Having dumped their cargoes at Berlin airfields, the aircraft would fly the needy to a safe haven, food and warmth at Lübeck which was under the control of the Allies.

So mammoth an undertaking was the Berlin airlift—the biggest transport operation ever—that aircraft accidents and casualties were inevitable; Flt. Lieut. Denyer had vivid memories of Allied planes and pilots that did not make it safely into the Berlin landing grounds. (During the airlift he was promoted from Flying Officer to Flt. Lieut.).

On one particular mission he remembers coming out of low cloud at

Gatow on final approach to land when he saw the final moments of a four-engine Avro York which crashed and finished up on the side of a hill: its cargo spewed out over the ground. Fortunately there was no fire and the crew escaped. The Avro York was the peace-time version of the famous Lancaster bomber. J.D. can recall other accidents on the Berlin run when Allied transport crashed coming into land in vile weather conditions; the most tragic of all concerned a plane load of German children which crashed into a wood during its landing approach into Lübeck. In all, nearly twenty RAF aircrew were killed during the airlift as well as numbers of other Allied fliers.

Jim was not involved in any air accidents though he did have one or two unnerving experiences. One was taking off from the Lübeck base with a full cargo for Berlin in a heavy snowstorm when the aircraft's electrical power failed. 'We lost radio contact and all lights inside the machine went out. Fortunately the second pilot had a torch at the ready and we pressed on though quick action was called for, with a stream of other aircraft behind…I was forced to turn towards the Russian zone to divert from other machines and to try and rectify the fault. That we failed to do. We had to wait for an eternity for the last aircraft to leave the stream before we could think about landing. We got down all right without running into any hostile Russian fighters.'

On another mission, returning to Lübeck from Berlin in freezing winter conditions during the night he discovered a problem with his tail-wheel as he taxied the DC-3 in. The wheel refused to castor; stopping the plane, J.D. found that the wheel was encased in a block of ice: 'I knocked it off and pushed it through the door of the flight operations room. I told a startled officer commanding night flying that until a few moments ago the ice-block had been part of my tail wheel!' Flying operations were then cancelled for the rest of the night.

The Berlin airlift was remarkable in the way that both pilots and planes stood up to the unrelenting task of flying in cargoes nonstop round the clock. It could not have got off the ground without the full co-operation of Britain, America, France and other European countries that supplied aircraft in great numbers as well as food and other commodities. To back up the airlift, commodities were also transported to British bases by road and rail for onward carriage to Berlin. One vital fuel, coal, came into the British bases from the Ruhr. The American Army Air Force, flying the airlift into Templehof in great numbers carried many thousands of tons of coal, food and other supplies into the stricken German capital.

Looking back on the Berlin airlift in 1993, J.D. was still awed by the size of this gigantic air transport operation, and the problems that had to be overcome. A major problem throughout was trying to operate a passenger plane efficiently as a makeshift cargo aircraft.

The Dakota was in reality the epoch-making American DC-3 airliner which had been built and introduced in the 1930s to carry some thirty passengers. That seems a tiny passenger aircraft now though in the 1930s it was the means of making commercial passenger carrying popular; it was so well designed with a high safety margin and easy handling that it can still be seen in the skies today.

In the end, the Allies won the 'Battle of Berlin'. In May, 1949, after more than 50,000 'mercy missions' flown into Berlin, and with the airlift at peak momentum, the Russians concluded that they could not win and lifted the blockade. Although the cost of the lift had been very considerable, and lives had been lost, the people of Berlin did not starve to death and could only celebrate the major reverse for the Soviets.

Only four years after the conclusion of a world war, pilots, navigators, radio operators and ground crews proved once again that the Royal Air Force was an élite force, manned by the most highly skilled airmen. And for one pilot, father of two children whose wife came from Newcastle, it was the end of an arduous and exhaustive operation that he would never forget.

1  Jim Denyer as a baby.
2  As a boy at primary school.

3  Experienced RAF fliers being trained as Instructors.

Commissioned as a Pilot Officer.
Alan Taylor in 'Mae West' lifesaver before a mission over enemy territory in his Mosquito.

6   Pilot Denyer in the cockpit of his Dakota during the Berlin airlift.
7   Jim Denyer's Mosquito.

8   1954. The first radar set at Newcastle Airport. Commandant Denyer adjusts the Decca 424
    Receiver, the first of its kind.

9   The plane that brought him to victory in 1956, Auster Autocrat G-AJRH. Jim Denyer
    favoured 'lucky 7'.

10 *National Air Races at Baginton, 1956. Winning the King's Cup for the first time, Jim Denyer is shouldered by Cyril Greory (right) and Beverley J. Snook (then chairman of the Royal Aero Club).*

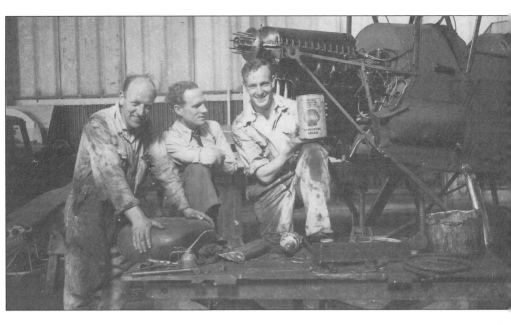

11 *The not so glamorous side of air racing. Jim Denyer with Allan Irwin, chief engineer (left) and Alec Imrie, in the fifties.*

12 *Jim Denyer's Tiger Moth which he called 'Victor Willie'. It made aviation history, the only Tiger Moth to have won the the premier air racing trophy.*

13  Jim Denyer seen here with his wife, Mary (right of picture), after winning the Norton Griffiths International Trophy (resting on top of the plane's fuselage.)

14  Double win for Jim Denyer in the 1958 air races. Michael Denyer (left) holds the King's Cup while Vivian Denyer grasps the Grosvenor International Trophy. In the background 'Victor Willie'.

15  *After winning the 1958 King's Cup.*

16  *Pilots of the Municipal Flying School, Newcastle, in the 1950s. Left to right:  Freddie Bain, Dave Davico (Chief Flying Instructor), Jim Denyer.*

The Canadair aircraft dumped at Newcastle Airport. Left to right: Jim Denyer, Abe Levy, the auctioneer.

18 Left to right: Jim Denyer, Lord Thomson, the late T. Dan Smith.

19 Ella Fitzgerald arriving at Woolsington in the 1960s.

20 Jim Denyer with the Lord Lieutenant (the late Duke of Northumberland), the Queen and Prince Philip.

1 *At the controls of a Dakota preparing for take-off.*
2 *Jim Denyer awarded the 'Geordie' passport.*

23 *Newcastle Airport Security Police, led by Chief Inspector Ray Irons, make a presentation to Jim Denyer in recognition of his service.*

4 'Queen of the Skies' Amy Johnson visits Cramlington Aerodrome, home of the Newcastle Aero Club, to be greeted by Mrs Baxter Ellis, wife of the Club chairman.

**e Flying Heppells.**

*P. Forsyth Heppell.*

*Philip Whaley Heppell.*

*Rhoda Heppell, later Fairbairn.*

28 The late Sheila Scott, first woman to fly round the world solo.

29 An outstanding woman pilot of the 1930s, Winifred Brown, receiving the magnificent Newcastle Air Trophy in 1930.

30 *A narrow escape for Jim Denyer in the 1960's. Flying passengers to Deauville for an air rally the crank-shaft of this Miles Messenger broke in mid-air, shearing off the propeller. They glided to safety at Brough Airfield.*

31 *Jim Denyer gives the thumbs up from the cockpit.*

32  *The end of an era for Jim at Newcastle, retiring in 1989. Seen here with John Donnelly, then chairman of the Airport Authority.*

33  *The Managing Director hands over responsibilty to his successor, Trevor Went.*

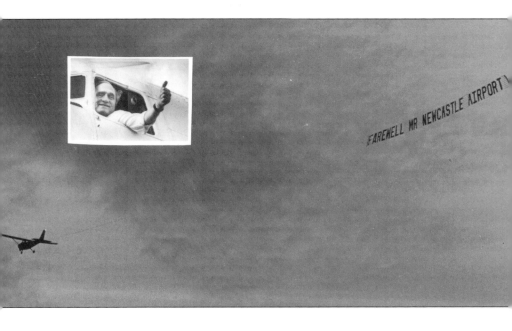

*The final flourish to the Woolsington farewell - a high-wing monoplane which flew from Teeside to weave the message through the sky: 'Farewell Mr. Newcastle Airport.'*

# Chapter V

## AIR RACING TRIUMPHS

## TWICE WINNER OF KING'S CUP

Like driving in Formula 1, powerboat racing and bobsleigh Olympics, competing in national air racing is a special experience. Even veteran pilots, coming to air racing after a lifetime of flying have been known to fall under its spell. The challenge of pushing a heavier than air machine at full throttle and minimum height round a very tight course releases the adrenalin, preparing the pilot for thrills and spills. Such a race is the King's Cup, the premier international air race, which Jim Denyer won twice from three starts.

This coveted trophy was presented by King George V in 1922 to improve the breed of British light aircraft machines and the pilots who flew them. Before the Second World War the race was a glorified cross-country event covering England in three days' flying. It began in the London area and worked its way north, one of the staging points being Newcastle upon Tyne. Suspended during the war, the race was revived in 1949 when King George VI gave a new cup to be competed for annually. A new format was introduced and for the next six years the National Air Races were staged over three separate meetings at different locations. Newcastle was the host airfield in 1952. But in 1956 a decision was taken to centre the whole of the races at Baginton, Coventry, with a four day competition proving a new attraction to the public.

From that time Britain's National Air Races went from strength to strength, and when Queen Elizabeth ascended to the throne, her wish was that the premier trophy of the week, the King's Cup, should continue to be known by that name.

It says something for the pilot skills and flying expertise of Jim Denyer that for fifteen years after the war he was the only aviator to have won the King's Cup twice. In 1960, the feat was equalled by another pilot.

The colour, hustle and bustle and air of excitement of national air racing days remained a vivid memory for Jim. On the day of the King's cup, he could easily recall how the tension mounts as the hour of the big race approaches. Some pilots go quiet; others huddle together in groups discussing the merits of the wind and weather; others become excited and crack jokes. The experienced flier like James H. Denyer keeps his own counsel, with an exact flight plan blue-printed in his mind that will give him the best possible chance of winning.

Some distance from the fliers stand the flying machines, not quite at the ready as engineers make final checks, and willing bands of helpers busy themselves waxing fuselages to allow polished surfaces to reduce friction and steal a fractional increase in the plane's speed. Every pilot searches for the most favourable handicap, working within race regulations. It has been known for a pilot to take a passenger into his racing aircraft to give him a better handicap. All aircraft taking part in the race are handicapped according to their known performance and history, the size and horse-power of their machine.

When J.D. won the first of his King's Cups in 1956, he was flying a standard Auster Autocrat from Newcastle Municipal Flying School which had been taken off training flights only two days before. Although there was little time for special preparation, the engineers worked flat out, knowing that the little machine was soon to be severely tested.

The national air race course at Baginton that day took the form of a quadrilateral, marked out by pylons about four miles apart. It was a tight course which was sure to provide a testing race for some of the country's best pilots.

The pattern of the race was determined by handicaps: the slowest machines were off first and the fastest last, in theory resulting in all machines reaching the finishing line within seconds of each other. J.D. had prepared well, but first he needed a fast take off, quickly reading the scatter points and locking onto course as rapidly as possible. His flight plan was to fly as low as possible over minimum safety height, preventing any time loss in climbing.

At last the time arrived to start his first King's Cup; the starter's flag dropped and pushing the monoplane to full throttle, he was away. He had a very good start and as he approached the first pylon marker, he turned his wing low to race round it. On the first two laps of the four lap race, he saw that the other fifteen racing machines were straddled out, though he knew they would come together in the final lap to stage a grandstand finish. Now he had to grapple with his first real problem—the onset of mist making visibility poor. He quickly decided to line the plane up on a known ground feature and wait for the next pylon turning point to emerge out of the mist.

With only two legs of the course remaining, there were still four competitors in front of him, though he was catching them quickly. As he overtook the leading machine on the final run in, he realised that he had a chance of a place though he was aware that he was being pursued by a gaggle of faster, more powerful aircraft. At that point he glanced down at the instruments on his control panel and noticed that his oil temperature gauge exceeded the maximum; 'I covered it up so that I could not see it and kept the machine at full throttle!' he recalled.

At top speed, he eased his aircraft into a shallow dive and made for the finishing line—passing it with his wheels only feet from the ground. He was aware that nothing had passed him and suddenly he experienced the elation that only victory brings; he had done it, he had won the most coveted air race of all by a margin of some ten seconds!

He had flown the race in his shirt-sleeves, but had to hurriedly don his club blazer when King Feisal of Iraq, guest of honour, asked him to go to the royal enclosure for a chat. After his spectacular win, the Newcastle pilot became headline news. His feat had been reported to the nation via Raymond Baxter and a BBC broadcast. The media did not know then that J.D. had only broken into air racing as a means of publicising Newcastle Airport.

Looking back on his first King's Cup triumph, he attributed his success to the superb low-level flying training he had received in the RAF; he was also grateful for the outstanding back-up service he got from his engineers and friends from the Newcastle Aero Club. The records show that J.D.'s first association with the National Air Races was not as a pilot but as an airport manager at Newcastle where the races were held in 1952. That was the first year of J.D.'s long reign as Airport Director, but unfortunately the event was marred by a most unusual incident at the start of the races.

Woolsington, in the early fifties, was a rather primitive airfield and on assuming command J.D. quickly introduced a runway improvement plan which involved laying a Tarmac surface on the grassy runway. It was a stroke of ill luck for the new manager that the work was not completed by the beginning of the air races. Tons of pit spoil had been laid on the old runway as under-fill but the tarmacadam was not in place. The engineers informed the authorities that if the spoil was solidly rolled in to provide a smooth surface for take-off, the runway could be used. That advice turned out to be optimistic in the extreme; it was to be exploded by the great force from the engines of a Vampire jet aircraft. When the Vampire taxied up to the start line, the pilot opened up his engines to full throttle to make a flying get away when the starter's flag fell. The result was a minor disaster. The blast from the jet ripped out great chunks of the runway and scattered spoil far and wide. J.D. can still picture the scene: 'Sections of the runway were flung towards Havannah Farm upon which a big black cloud settled. The farmer was not best pleased as the explosion covered the roof of his farmhouse with brown dirt.' It says much for the coolness of the jet aircraft pilot that he took off all right, although he was fortunate he could not see the devastation he wrought behind him! By the time he was airborne, the slowest, propeller-driven machines had already covered three laps of the four lap race. Turning on the speed, the Vampire jet still came in third. The comments of Field Marshall Montgomery, who made the prize presentations, are not recorded.

Jim made his debut in air racing in 1955 and what a year it turned out to be. In his first ever race—held at Fairwood Common, Swansea, in unusual circumstances—he was successful. That former RAF airfield, which by then had reverted back to common land with public access, caused pilots all sorts of problems. Flocks of sheep had to be cleared from the landing field, and daredevil youngsters riding cycles and motorbikes raced alongside aircraft as they took off and landed!

The start of the race was hectic to say the least. J.D. and two other pilots, all without handicap had to draw lots for position in a formation take-off. That resulted in frantic jockeying for position at the start of the race. At the end of the first lap the Newcastle pilot had thrust himself in front and was never headed, capturing the Norton Griffiths International Trophy. In his Flying school Tiger Moth he had accumulated more points than any other pilot after three races.

Later in 1955, entering another meeting of the national air races at Bristol, he witnessed an amazing escape from an aircraft which crashed immediately in front of him. The pilot, Beverley Snook, whom Jim was overtaking in the final lap of the race, hit the ground with his aircraft, causing it to somersault and finish upside down. After Jim had flashed past him to the finishing line, he parked his own plane and dashed to the scene of the crash. 'I was amazed to see Bev standing there having made an escape from the wrecked plane. He just stood in his white overalls and said to me nonchalantly: "Some bugger has pinched my packet of cigarettes!!"' Pilot Snook's amazing escape was due to the fact that he was held to his seat by straps as the plane somersaulted, the top wing acting as protection against his head. Later in his career he was elected chairman of the Royal Aero Club.

For Jim the year 1955 went out on a high note when he finished runner-up in the British Air Racing Championship. By this time he was caught under the spell of air racing and infected by the magic conjured up by national air race competition. One way and another he was often involved in high drama. The year 1957 was no exception and the race was a heat for the Goodyear Challenge Trophy. When the race day broke over Baginton Airfield conditions were far from perfect. It was cold and cloudy with outbreaks of rain. The gusty wind was at times troublesome. Nevertheless, Jim managed to become involved in a sensational finish. When he came to the finishing line in his Auster machine he was flying neck-and-neck with a Miles Monarch piloted by W.P. Bowles, a London businessman. Race officials could not separate them; they declared a dead-heat. Bowles went on to win the final. Experienced pilots and officials said at the time that they had seen nothing like it before. Chief Race Executive, Col. R.L. 'Mossy' Preston said: 'I am sure that it has never happened in an air race before.' (Jim recalls that Col. Preston was a real character and behind his back he was affectionately known as 'Stromboli' because his waistcoat was invariably covered in cigarette ash!).

So the air racing season of 1957 came to a close, and J.D. could hardly wait for the new season to begin—though he could not have foreseen the triumphs that lay in waiting in 1958.

First, he entered and won the national event for the Grosvenor Challenge Trophy; and then, for the second time in three years, he captured the greatest prize of all, the King's Cup. But there is a story which suggests that 'Lady Luck' was smiling on J.H. Denyer that year. Flying the qualifying rounds at Baginton, which would climax with the running of the King's Cup he was at the controls of the same blue Tiger Moth that he had raced successfully in the Norton Griffiths Trophy in 1955, though the plane had been modified. It had one cockpit instead of two, and other streamlining modifications had been carried out. In order to get the plane ready for the major race event, the Newcastle aircraft engineers, under Bob Forsyth, worked all hours. Despite the great effort put in to prepare the plane J.D. failed to qualify for the King's Cup by one place. He thought his chance to win had gone. Then fate stepped in and overnight he found himself lining up with the competitors for the King's Cup after all. His inclusion was the result of a most unusual circumstance. John Pothecary, an airline pilot who had qualified to race for the King's Cup,was recalled to duty by his airline at very short notice allowing the twenty-first qualifier, Jim Denyer, to take his place. What followed was one of the hardest-fought races ever. Flying Tiger Moth G-AIVW powered by a DH Gypsy Major lc engine, he was last off in his handicap class.

In the hectic final run in, he had overtaken all the planes in his class while other faster aircraft were closing behind him. As Jim saw it that day: 'As the tail of my plane crossed the finishing line I saw two faster aircraft flash past me. I thought I was beaten into third place. In fact officials informed me that I had won by 1.2 seconds! '

A further success in the national races of that year was winning the Lord Grosvenor Trophy as the fastest aircraft in the Tiger Moth class, a fitting finale for the racing year of 1958, closing on another high note.

What was the secret of Jim's amazing success in the first few years of national air racing? And what kind of an experience was it? He described it thus: 'The thrill of low-level racing around pylon markers is difficult to explain; you had to fly so very accurately otherwise you plunged into the ground. Air racing is very exciting and stimulating, and it's something that gets into your blood once you start. My technique was to find the highest point of the course in practice and never to fly above that in the race itself. I used to clip across tops of trees at the highest point. When conditions were right, I used to fly round pylons at eighty degrees with my lower wing some twenty feet off the ground. It was a dangerous business, but if you flew to plan you could reduce the time allowed by the handicapper for your aircraft. There was a lot to air racing; one all-important factor was judging the wind direction and strength in order to calculate the start and finish of a turn.'

The reality of the dangers of air racing came home to roost one year at Yeadon, Yorkshire, when he nearly 'bought it'. In the second race of that day he was involved in a mass start of planes, nine aircraft, of which he was last, taking off within fifteen seconds. The alarm bells rang at the first turning point of the race. Flying about thirty feet off the ground in a steep turn round a pylon he was strongly buffeted by slipstreams from aircraft in front of him. He takes up the story: 'I was flipped straight onto my back. Instinct made me continue with the roll. I did not try and stop it and straighten up. Had I done that, I would have been dead. I kept the stick hard over and finished the roll. It was all over in the fraction of a second.'

What an escape that was, flying so close to the ground. In fact it was the first time any pilot had rolled an aircraft over at thirty feet in the national air races! Even after that, Jim gave his machine everything it had got, and finished second.

After the racing triumphs in the years up to 1958, the next two years were only moderately successful for the Newcastle flier who found that the development of his airport was taking all his time. In the national air races of 1959, switching back to an Auster Autocrat (the sister aircraft of the winner of the 1956 King's Cup) he was again winner of the Norton Griffiths International Trophy. That qualified him, once more, to compete in the King's Cup. On this occasion, luck deserted him. On the third circuit of the big race he lost power and the engine started rough-running. That happened at a critical time after negotiating a pylon turn which headed him and his machine towards a wood. Danger stared him in the face. He decided to shut the engine down and carry out a forced landing. He turned away from the wood and was heading towards a field of oats with a narrow passage between two trees. Jim remembers: 'I went in sideways, straightened up and slid through the trees, putting the plane down in field of oats. If I had missed landing between those trees I was dead.'

Airfield officials, alerted to the fact that Pilot Denyer was missing, radioed other pilots in the race to keep a lookout. One pilot picked up the missing Auster in the oatfield and radioed back to the airfield: 'I have picked up the Auster in the oatfield, the pilot looks to be all right, I can see his jockey cap moving through the oats!' Jim discovered that his 'full-throttle' flying in a bid to win had over-heated the oil in the engine. 'I was accused of over-enthusiastic throttle-bending!' he said.

The final episode in his racing career ended in disappointment. From the beginning of the 1960 national air races, flying a borrowed plane which had not been finely tuned, he was handicapped out of it. 'I was flying a slow machine, a Tiger Moth carrying a severe handicap, I didn't stand a cat in hell's chance of winning anything.' So the final curtain fell on the short but drama-filled career of James H. Denyer as an air racer. Summing it up, he said 'I have to say that in six short years I probably achieved more than most people who have been competing for a lifetime.' No one could argue with that.

When he left air racing, he took with him a much prized memento in the form of the Tiger Club Medal. For Jim, along with other pilots, the Hon. Peter Vanneck (sometime Euro MEP for a North East constituency), Basil Maile, Beverley Snook and Norman Jones, was a founder member of this exclusive racing club. The Tiger Club, internationally known, was first thought of at the Yeadon races of 1955. Its special logo, designed by national newspaperman Chris Wren, was painted on the fuselage of member machines, a source of pride, envied by others.

In later years, Norman Jones, a wealthy businessman financed the extension of activities of the club which, by the mid 1960s was the only aviation organisation to stage a regular 'Flying Circus' round the country. It was then based at Redhill Aerodrome, Surrey, and was open to pilots with more than one hundred hours flying in command provided they had expertise in air racing or aerobatics. Several famous names in flying were associated with the Tiger Club including Sheila Scott, the first European to fly round the world solo. Norman Jones' contribution to flying was immense. After starting the Tiger Aero Club at Redhill, he opened a flying training school offering cheap rates of instruction, presenting the opportunity to fly to the less well off.

Denyer won a reputation during his racing years for flying flat out during a race, as a result of which he was invited to join another exclusive body of racing pilots called 'The Throttle Benders Union'. Members displayed an appropriate logo on the engine cowling of their aircraft.

If the racing pilots were the 'glamour boys' of the air, then the aircraft engineers were the 'hidden geniuses' of air racing. Unless the engineers produced an aircraft finely tuned in first-class condition and preparedness, it stood no chance of winning 'the big one'. That is why Jim, looking back, was the first to pay tribute to the skills of the engineers at Newcastle Flying School, without whom he could not have had such success.

As well as helping to win all Jim Denyer's trophies, the Newcastle engineers also prepared aircraft that won the Goodyear Trophy (pilot, Stan Jours) and the British Air Racing Championship (pilot, Sqn. Ldr. Jimmy Rush) in the 1950s. As Jim summed it up: 'That is a very remarkable record and illustrates the high standard of engineering skills by the Newcastle team.'

# Chapter VI

## NEWCASTLE AIRPORT: THE GENESIS

## BEGINNING OF AN EPOCH

W hen Newcastle opened its airport for operations in 1935, James H. Denyer was a boy of twelve living in Kent with no connections with Tyneside. Little did he know that in only eight years' time he would be a war-time RAF pilot at Ouston, that he would meet the girl he would marry at RAF Woolsington, and that his career would launch a major international airport for the North East.

If fate decreed that he should play no part in the airport opening, he more than made up for it in the last forty years; and possessing a zest for local aviation history there is little he did not know about the history of Newcastle Airport.

In a downstairs room in his Ponteland bungalow stands a tall, steel filing-cabinet which is crammed full of dossiers, memoranda, booklets and brochures, press cuttings and photographs which tell the story of the emergence of Newcastle Airport. For example one can dip into the Woolsington treasure-chest and pull out the original official programme of opening day in July 1935. Exactly at noon on Friday 26 July the Secretary of State for Air, Sir Philip Cunliffe-Lister declared the airport open.

At the time of a great slump when more than 2,000,000 people were out of work and the North was the hardest hit, the Air Minister had no doubt that the City's cash was being wisely spent. 'It is particularly creditable that you have carried it through on sound lines with a view to future development, when I know your area has been stricken by the depression', he said.

Reading the souvenir programme the new airport sounded very grand. 'The club-house contains a large lounge, dining room, hall, buffet, sanitary conveniences for both sexes. Residential accommodation is provided for the steward, and sleeping quarters are available for a limited number of visitors. Hangar, workshops, offices, ambulance room, store for petrol and oil supply, garage for fire tender and sewage disposal plant have been installed'.

In reality that was rather a glossy description of the the aerodrome which consisted mainly of a building, a hangar and a grassy strip. Presented to the Air Minister that day was a power of a man, Sir Stephen Easten whose herculean efforts as chairman of the Municipal Aerodrome Committee had forced the building of the airport through; and J.D. Irving, the respected chairman of Newcastle Aero Club who had signed an agreement making the Aero Club managers of the new venture.

That opening day was to be memorable for two flying displays: the highly-disciplined display of aerobatics given by an RAF flight and the highly entertaining trick-flying given by the Alan Cobham 'flying circus'.

The Royal Air Force display was given by pilots and machines from the Central Flying School, Wittering. A display of RAF aerobatics, including formation flying was a rare occasion fifty years ago, the daring of the professional pilots bringing gasps of amazement from the large crowd. The Avro single engine biplanes looped, half rolled, downward looped and turning upside down flew in formation, much to the thrill of onlookers. The appetite whetted, a second display of trick flying was led by one of the famous aviators of his time, Sir Alan Cobham, whose pioneering feats included opening up air routes to countries in the British Empire like India, Australia and South Africa.

Although this was a memorable day for Sir Stephen Easten, his ceaseless striving to establish a local airport coupled with running a large, successful building business had taken its toll and he was already a sick man. Unfortunately he would be dead a year later. Sir Stephen and his followers had had to win over the doubters who pointed fingers at an area wracked by unemployment, where some people were existing on near-starvation diets and were so poor they could not pay taxes. Some councillors argued that the £35,000 that the airport was costing could have been put to better use. In the year that the airport received its first licence, after twelve months' satisfactory operation, the Jarrow Marchers set off to London.

Papers from the Denyer 'library' tell you that the story of Newcastle Airport actually begins in 1929, a quarter of a century after the first flight by the Wright Brothers, and twenty years after Bleriot crossed the Channel. The idea was prompted by the Air Ministry, an indication that Government was aware of the need to push aviation in Britain forward in light of progress being made by other European countries.

The immediate reaction among Newcastle councillors was one of hostility. Ald. Joseph Stephenson referred to an obvious choice for an airfield and declared that the location of the Town Moor should not be entertained. It was a valuable piece of moorland close to the city and much used by citizens for sport and leisure. Other councillors argued: 'How can you spend so much money on an aerodrome when people all over the city are hungry and cold for want of money.'

However, after much debate there were enough aldermen and councillors in favour of establishing an aerodrome somewhere in Newcastle to win the day. The supporters, led by Ald. Sir George Lunn pointed out the growing importance of aviation and argued that Newcastle could not afford to be left behind. The first concrete step was taken when

Newcastle City Council agreed to 'investigate the question of building a municipal aerodrome for Newcastle', though the Lord Mayor made it clear that the Town Moor could not be considered as a site.

The year 1929 was a significant date for many local municipalities considering establishing aerodromes of their own. One of the most active boroughs was Sunderland who were recommended by the Air Ministry to consider a site at White Mare Pool, Boldon. Although a chartered civil engineer reported favourably on that site, it was turned down by first Sunderland and later, after the war, by Newcastle who were looking at possible sites for a new regional airport.

With hindsight, this could have made a fine regional airport today. It was situated almost equidistant from Newcastle, South Shields and Sunderland; the site of 200 acres was on the then main Ferryhill-London LNE line with good road links, plus a projected new road to the south linking up with Teesside. The plan as drawn up in 1929 was for the provision of three runways, of 7,000, 5,000 and 4,000 feet with the capability of extension later—which would have made it one of the most modern airports in the country. Critics argued against the very high cost and the fact that the site suffered from limited visibility, resulting from industrial haze. They also pointed to mining subsidence.

By 1931 Newcastle Aerodrome Committee engaged the services of Alan Cobham to carry out an aerial survey of eighteen possible sites. Later, after presenting his report the City Council decided that land at High House Farm, Woolsington was the best prospect. The land covered 345 acres of which 107 acres would be required for the airfield, leaving land immediately available for expansion. The site was some six miles from Newcastle Central Station which could be traversed by car in only fifteen minutes.

Jim Denyer recalled that when work eventually began on the land in 1934 to flatten, harrow and sow with seed, a special kind of seed was bought in from Russia. That was three years hence; there was much delay ahead. First the City Council, strapped for cash, discovered that no Government grants would be available to contribute towards cost of development. Further, air travel was not commercially viable and the City of Newcastle was bound to lose money. Then the Ministry for Civil Aviation threw a spanner into the works by turning down the application to build an airport on the Woolsington site. The Ministry's refusal was based on a report from the Government Mineral Valuer who drew attention to adjacent coal-mining operations which could cause subsidence.

The projected site was virtually surrounded by coal-mining; mining leases had been granted to work six adjacent seams, and mining operations had already started to the south and east of the site. Coal-mining would take place under Woolsington in between three and five years' time after which the Coal Board planned continuous mining operations. That, said the Ministry, would create considerable and uneven subsidence making Woolsington unsuitable for aerodrome development. They told Newcastle to look for another site.

Newcastle Aerodrome Committee wholeheartedly rejected the Ministry decision. They had already spent much money in inspecting eighteen sites and coming to a local decision. Ald. Stephen Easten told the City Council that the danger from subsidence was 'greatly exaggerated' and that subsidence from mining operations was taking place, to some degree or other, all over the district. In January, 1933 the City Council engaged a local mining engineer, Col. Frank Simpson to inspect the site and make an independent report.

After a survey, he declared Woolsington suitable for development provided no further mining operations were begun in the area. That result was communicated to the Ministry who at first refused then, three months later, gave the airport development the green light. No explanation from the Ministry is recorded in the City Council minutes; the only clue is a reference to the Northern Group of MPs taking up the issue with the Minister. It looked as though political pressure was successfully brought to bear.

The year was 1934 before the purchase of land from the Meek Brothers, farmers of High House Farm, had been completed, and before work on the site began. Who were the people who made local history by building the aerodrome? Another dip into the Denyer archives shows the following companies were involved:

Laying out and developing the site—the En-Tout-Cas Co. of Syston, Leicester.
Constructing the approach road—McLaren and Co. of Belford.
Installing the water main—Rowells (1924) Ltd of Newcastle.
Laying electrical cables—the NE Electrical Supply Co. of Newcastle.
Supplying the fire tender—Northern Coach Builders of Newcastle.
Erecting airfield fencing—Calders Ltd of North Shields.

The buildings architect was Sydney Wilson of Hetherington and Wilson of Newcastle, and works direction was by the City Engineer, and officials of Newcastle Aero Club. The Aero Club was in debt to Sir Stephen Easten who presented them with a solidly built clubhouse which is still in use today. In that key period of development, guiding hands were provided by members of the Aero Club Committee which included Sir Joseph Reed (President), J.D. Irving (chairman) John Boyd (a Newcastle solicitor), Forsyth Heppell and Arthur George (a Newcastle motor trader). They were given the task of managing the airport on behalf of the Corporation.

The new aerodrome featured a wireless operations room, the embryo of today's air traffic control; while on the ground in the centre of the airfield the name NEWCASTLE was emblazoned in white painted concrete blocks as a means of of identification. The erection of the aerodrome hangar and other outbuildings cost some £1,200. Because nightflying was very limited—and the cost was high—the Corporation elected not to install an electrical flare-path. J.D. recalled that the Aero Club was responsible for providing petrol and pumps for refuelling aircraft, and also for providing food and lodging for crews and passengers. The Aero Club, while acting as airport manager, would also continue to run a flying training school.

The final cost of preparing the site and erecting the buildings totalled £33,117 (to which had to be added the cost of supplying equipment and back-up services). The Corporation was aware that the new aerodrome would lose money in the early years. The deficit forecast for the first year's working was £2,636 of which £2,000 went in repaying loan charges.

If the days of mass air travel, package holidays and everyday air freighting lay in the distant future, Newcastle had taken the plunge arguing that they could not be left behind other cities like Manchester, Liverpool and Hull.

Newcastle had strong support from the Newcastle and Gateshead Incorporated Chamber of Commerce to establish an airport. In 1934 the Chamber added new dynamism to the campaign when they appointed Leslie Runciman as chairman of the Chamber's Aviation Committee. Runciman, of Chathill, Northumberland and member of the well-known Runciman shipping dynasty, was a brilliant pilot and one of the pioneers of civil flying in Newcastle. He had established the first aircraft company at Cramlington, the headquarters of the Newcastle Aero Club by the late 1920s, and was a winner in national air races in the 1930s. His vision was to establish one large, modern airport for the North East region. In the end he failed to unite North East local authorities, while Newcastle was already sold on the Woolsington site. Runciman, in the 1932 King's Cup Air Race, piloting a DH Puss Moth won the Siddeley Trophy for the first club-trained pilot past the winning post.

So by 1935, Newcastle Airport was up and running. A company called North East Airways advertised that they could fly businessmen from Newcastle to London in just two and a half hours. Arriving at Croydon, passengers then had to board bus or rail which would take a further hour to reach the centre of London. This inaugural flight was scheduled from Croydon to Perth (and return) with a stop at Newcastle to pick up fuel and passengers.

The air versus rail battle for passengers started in earnest when the old London and North Eastern Railway introduced their crack express, the *Flying Scotsman* on the East Coast mainline, substantially reducing duration of journeys. Nevertheless, North East Airways continued to operate with some success until the 1939-45 war intervened; their beautiful flying machines, the de Havilland Rapides and the Airspeed Envoys, were popular with passengers.

During World War II, Woolsington played its part as an RAF Station, though it never buzzed to the feats of the fighter squadrons, the 'Spits' and the 'Hurries.' Its main roles were operating No. 83 Maintenance Unit—supporting the active fighter base at Ouston—and running the RAF Salvage Unit for crashed aircraft. At one point of the war, Anson and Walrus machines carried out coastal patrols from Woolsington.

When armistice was declared the airport site was handed back to Newcastle Corporation in 1946. Little development took place in the next half dozen years. That was unsurprising. The country was reeling from the great economic strain imposed by a world war; the regeneration of business and exporting was to take some time; and post-war passengers still preferred mass-travel by rail or road. To add to airport post-war problems, the Labour Government swept to power and announced plans to nationalise civil aviation. That state of affairs was little changed when J.H. Denyer was appointed Commandant of the Airport in August, 1952. Apart from a wooden control tower and a few Nissen huts, the appearance was similar to that other great opening day in July, 1935. Details of early Woolsington and its first licence have been securely held all through the years in a finely crafted wooden cylinder. One little surprise (the author was permitted to open the cylinder) was that for some reason the Air Ministry had located Newcastle Airport at Kenton (not Woolsington) in 1935. The theory is that Kenton was inserted as Government buildings were located there. In fact the first full licence was not issued until 1936 as Woolsington had to undergo a period of probation. One of its operating conditions was that the airfield had to be 'adequately equipped to extricate persons from wrecked aircraft.' The Ordnance Survey map which accompanied the licence is piece of local history in itself; High House Farm stands only just outside the perimeter amid unspoilt countryside; close by are Woolsington Hall and stables, kennels and pheasantry. To the south east lay the South Gosforth-Ponteland NE Railway branch line, with a pickup at Callerton Station.

# Chapter VII

## A NEW MANAGER FOR NEWCASTLE AIRPORT

## JAMES H. DENYER TAKES UP THE CHALLENGE

The year 1952 was a landmark in the history of Newcastle Airport. It heralded the appointment of James H. Denyer as Commandant and was the beginning of an association, pregnant with challenge and testing times, that was to last for at least the first decade. When he sat down behind the manager's desk for the first time that August morning more than forty years ago, he was under no illusion about the size of the task ahead. He had numerous priorities, though two urgent developments had to be started at once: to persuade airline companies to inaugurate scheduled services from Newcastle and to publicise the 'unknown' airport called Woolsington.

The drive and determination of the new manager brought early success—a company with local links, Hunting Air Transport, agreed to start services to London and other destinations, although they began in a small way, operating the proven old warhorse, the Dakota with a seating capacity of thirty passengers, and the slightly bigger twin-engine Viking, which was faster than the Dakota. After Hunting amalgamated with the Clan Shipping Line to form Hunting Clan, they introduced the superior Vickers Viscount, continuing scheduled flights from Newcastle to London, Belfast, Amsterdam and Düsseldorf. Hunting Clan did not, however, remain at Woolsington for much longer, opting for more lucrative work abroad. In 1955, their network of services was split between two airlines; Silver City (from Blackpool) operated the plum service to Amsterdam and Düsseldorf, while Dragon Airways flew to Manchester, Belfast and Dublin using DH Heron and Dove aircraft. The London route was awarded to BKS Air Charter which changed its name to BKS Air Transport. That airline had something of a fairytale beginning. In the early 1950s when the local subsidiary, the Lancashire Aircraft Corporation closed down, three former employees formed a partnership. They called themselves BKS Air Charter, BKS being the initials of the surnames of the three partners: Jim Barnby (an accountant), Mike Keegan (an aircraft engineer) and John Stevens (a pilot). They started life operating charters in Africa. Then, making enough money to buy a second aircraft, began holiday services, extending only as far as the Channel Islands. This small, go-ahead company was part of the embryo operation which eventually blossomed out into the great package holiday market. Charlie Jackson was BKS manager, assisted by Dick Barton, sales.

In 1959 they were joined by a young man called Jim Shields who through the years has become part of the legend of Newcastle Airport, rising to become British Airways Manager.

The BKS logo became familiar to considerable numbers of Tyneside businessmen who took advantage of their scheduled flights to London. The airline introduced the beautiful forty-four-seater Elizabethan aircraft (earlier known as the Ambassador), then the Vickers Viscount followed by the popular Britannia, known affectionately as 'The Whispering Giant'. By this time, the network of schedule services from Newcastle had split between BKS Air Transport and Silver City, which became part of British United Airways.

By 1960, a new momentum in passenger movement through Newcastle had begun; passenger traffic had increased from a low of 5,000 passengers in 1952 to more than 119,000 in 1960. That year another airline arrived in Newcastle which was to witness a long love affair with the local airport—Dan-Air Services. Since that time, Dan-Air have been the most consistent network operator to fly schedule services from Newcastle (see postscript). In those early days, the company pioneered an international route to Norway, and on the domestic front a new service to the West Country. On the personnel front, another Denyer was to arrive at Woolsington in the sixties: Viv Denyer ( a son of J.D.) started as a clerk in Air Traffic Control and is still there today as an ATC Supervisor.

By 1971, Dan-Air, part of Davies and Newman Holdings, a well-established London company of shipping brokers, was operating a 'Link City' service between Newcastle, Liverpool, Manchester, Bristol and Cardiff. The aircraft used was the Nord 262. Two years later, Dan-Air had opened up the Newcastle-Gatwick service in direct competition with British Airways, the new giant carrier formed in 1972 of which BKS Air Services had formed a part.

For many years, the Newcastle to London link has been the 'bread and butter' run for British Airways—even twenty years ago the company was transporting 250,000 passengers per year into their Heathrow Terminal. In spite of that dominance, by 1976 Dan-Air had 50,000 passengers on their Newcastle-Gatwick connection. Unfortunately, years later Dan-Air was to run into serious financial trouble, resulting in their eventual demise.

Another prestige airline to come to Newcastle in the mid-sixties was British Caledonian, an amalgamation of the major Scottish carrier, Caledonian Airways, and British United. Continuing fast, schedule services into Schipol, Amsterdam, the airline upped the frequency from three departures a week to three a day within the first decade of starting the operation. Schipol Airport attracted North Eastern businessmen and industrialists, providing speedy links to all corners of the globe with its multifarious leading airlines and extensive international schedule services.

The introduction of the jet airliner in the 1960s made a great impact on air travel. The jets, far faster than the previous piston engine aircraft, radically reduced journey times. The boost to passenger traffic at Woolsington occurred in 1969 when the three main schedule network operators changed from piston and turbo-prop engines to the latest pure jet aircraft.

In that year, Dan-Air bought BAC-1-11 jets to supplement their Comet fleet and to replace the faithful Ambassador/Elizabethans. Also flying the BAC-1-11 to Amsterdam in the 1970s was British Caledonian. By the beginning of the 1970s, the new airport had well and truly entered the jet age. Although J.D. was successful in attracting new airline services to Newcastle during his first decade, he was powerless to improve the image of Woolsington. All through the 1950s and early 1960s he wrestled with this problem, aware that businessmen flying in from London and Europe would be less than impressed with the old wooden huts that served as offices and the airport terminal.

The airport manager was under pressure from north-eastern industrialists to modernise the airport, but the problem was that no single local authority, not even Newcastle, could provide the vast sums of money to build a modern terminal complex with its attendant services. Newcastle Corporation, the owners of the airport, aware that there was no Government money in the form of grants to assist development, realised that the answer was to form a consortium of North East local authorities. Yet when Newcastle's Town Clerk, John Atkinson, asked more than twenty local authorities to join them to thrust Newcastle into the forefront of modern aviation, the response was lukewarm. 'There was little enthusiasm from them,' recalls J.D. 'They were not convinced that Woolsington was the right and proper location for the regional airport.' During that period of the fifties, there was opposition too from numbers of Newcastle City Councillors who argued against funding a new airport complex when money was sorely needed by other Newcastle City services.

There was another major problem which the airport manager had to grapple with at this period—the spectre of mining subsidence reappeared to haunt Woolsington once again. The trouble came to light in 1957, and the Newcastle Airport Committee was informed that serious subsidence had occurred on the east west runway and demanded immediate attention.

Following inspection and surveys, the City Engineer estimated that the cost of resettling the runway was £7,500. As if that were not enough, the Airport Committee was then informed that the National Coal Board had applied to mine 35,000 tons of coal lying in a seam under or close to the airport buildings. Newcastle Corporation lost little time in approaching the Coal Board to express their gravest misgivings about the mining project. The Coal Board assured the Corporation that they would pay compensation for any damage caused by mining! The fact was that the Coal Board, under licence, had been mining the Woolsington area for years; and it was going to take another six years before the spectre of mining at Woolsington was finally exorcised.

This incredible story which launched one commercial interest against another was to run and run. In one way or another manager Denyer was to grapple with the ramifications of mining subsidence from the day he took over the airport in 1952. When he was appointed Airport Commandant in that year, he discovered there were four main seams running close to the airport. They were the Beaumont Seam, the Busty Seam, the Brockwell Seam, and the Low Main Seam (which was nearest the surface).

While the main runway remained unaffected until 1957, J.D. could never put mining subsidence completely out of his mind. In fact the coal working, which out-cropped onto the airfield itself, was plainly visible to airport staff. Below ground a number of Bell-type workings were found in land adjacent to the airport. Under the Bell mining system, a sunken vertical shaft branched out into seams which extended laterally into a circle. The risk to the airfield through subsidence demanded that these workings be filled in. As J.D. recalled: 'On taking over at Newcastle Airport I discovered that it was not unusual engineering practice to build over unstable land, though I was shaken to a degree when I found out it could happen to an airfield.' When parts of the airfield started to slip, subsidence could be seen in a number of areas—for example the hangar doors would not close properly. J.D. remembered: 'During the early years when I used to go round speaking to different organisations in my campaign to publicise the airport, I used to joke about the position of the Low Main Seam in relation to the airfield surface. I quipped that if you put your ear to the surface about noon you could hear the miners munching their bait below!'

The biggest problem appeared in March, 1960 when a dish opened up on the main runway, sinking two or three feet down over a distance of 150 metres. It happened virtually overnight and was like a large saucer in the runway. Together with Capt. Jack Jessop, an experienced Elizabethan pilot J.D. carried out inspections and they agreed the dish was at take-off point for aircraft. J.D. continues the story: 'We informed all pilots flying from Newcastle, and with full knowledge of the problem they said they would continue to fly out services. Aircraft taking off would accelerate down the runway and, by the time they entered the dip, had reached velocity one to rotate, thus launching themselves clear of the dip and into take-off. It wasn't dangerous provided that the pilots of the Elizabethans, fitted with a front nosewheel, were aware of it. 'There were no complaints from passengers as they knew nothing.'

The airport manager decided to go for lightning repair. 'The plan was for work to start as soon as the last aircraft had landed on the Friday night, work nonstop over the whole weekend and complete by the Monday morning. When I informed the City Engineer, he nearly had a fit!' George Leigh, one of the City Engineer's surveyors rushed up to the airport and after inspecting the damage said 'Right Jim, we'll do it.'

The operation had to be seen to be believed. Steam-rollers fitted with scarifiers tore up a section of the runway and a fleet of thirty wagons ran a shuttle service of loads of pit-spoil as new infill. When the dish was filled in, it was hard rolled and base course of Tarmac applied. 'The workmen were marvellous and the fantastic operation was completed in time for airline services to begin on the Monday morning, though I didn't sleep the whole week-end. We applied the top course of Tarmac to the runway the following weekend.'

Unfortunately for J.D. the problem of mining subsidence would not go away. A year later, in November 1961 the City Engineer reported a rather alarming state of affairs: large scale mining had now begun in the area of the airport. Four different seams, down to a depth of 670 feet were being worked, and the Coal Board intended to continue extracting coal until 1967.

Repairs to airfield faults caused by subsidence had now cost Newcastle Corporation some £33,000 — about the same sum that it had cost to build the whole of the new airport at Woolsington in 1935. By 1963, when the problem of mining operations was settled and brought to a halt, the bill facing Newcastle was over £43,000.

The fight by Newcastle and later by the new North East Regional Airport Committee to stop the mining and claim compensation turned into a protracted battle. The 'big showdown' came in the 1960s when the Regional Airport Committee, under chairman, Andy Cunningham, met the Coal Board under Lord Robens. When the Airport Committee demanded compensation for all the repairs carried out to the Woolsington airfield, the Coal Board countered with a demand for the North East Regional Airport Committee to pay for their loss of profit on unmined sterilised coal on the site. 'It came to a verbal bout of fisticuffs. I remember that Lord Robens and his boffins walked out of the meeting held in Durham. Andy Cunningham said "let them simmer down, they'll come back in". They did, and in the end an agreement was reached and I believe that little or no money exchanged hands. The parties agreed that the loss of profit on unmined coal deposits roughly equalled the cost of repairs carried out by first Newcastle and then the Regional Airport Authority.'

As Lord Hailsham, Minister for the North at the time, threw his considerable weight behind the case for the region, declaring that the development of Newcastle Airport should not be impeded, victory was assured.

All mining operations in the Woolsington area ceased—and one airport manager heaved a sigh of relief.

# Chapter Vlll

## INTO THE SIXTIES

## MAJOR DEVELOPMENTS AT WOOLSINGTON

## A NEW TERMINAL AT LAST

The catalyst that resulted in the birth of the powerful North East Regional Airport Committee was released at a meeting in London between Newcastle Corporation and a senior Government Minister in 1958. This new Committee, supported by money from five local authorities in the region was to be the launch pad for the building of a new terminal building complex at Woolsington which would thrust the area into the forefront of modern aviation.

The Minister was John Boyd-Carpenter, Secretary for Transport, who told the Corporation representatives—for the first time—that there was Government money in the pipeline for Newcastle. He introduced a qualification though: before he could authorise a capital grant towards the cost of a new terminal, he would have to be told that the North East had formed a Regional Airport Committee.

Col. Robert Mould-Graham, chairman of Newcastle's Airport Committee and Jim Denyer, airport manager left the meeting with the Minister in high spirits. Furnished with the promise of Government money, all that remained was to bring the region's local authorities together. Once again, Newcastle discovered that this was a difficult road to go down; the authorities were slow to respond and in fact it took until 1963 before five of the North East local authorities united to form the first Regional Airport Committee.

In the end, it was intense pressure and lobbying by the region's businessmen and industrialists that knocked heads together and brought about a first meeting. Even then, only five local authorities were persuaded to join the North East Regional Airport Committee: Newcastle, Gateshead, South Shields, and Northumberland and Durham Counties. Tynemouth and Sunderland joined the Committee after a time, bringing the strength of the North East consortium to seven. It was ominous that when the Regional Airport Committee met for the first time in 1963, no Teesside Authority was in sight; they were occupied with thoughts of forming their own Committee to launch a separate Teesside Airport.

The first meeting of the Regional Airport Committee, called at Newcastle's Town Hall got off to an explosive start. As Jim Denyer remembers it, the other big player in the negotiations, Durham County Council, was prepared to let Newcastle lead the consortium with Dr Henry Russell in the chair. Though when the Durham contingent of councillors, led by Ald. Andy Cunningham arrived at the Town Hall they were ushered into an assembly room to await the presence of John Atkinson, the Newcastle Town Clerk. The latter informed Ald. Cunningham, 'Alderman Russell would like you to come down to his office, he wants to have a talk with you.' According to Mr Denyer: 'that message was like a red rag to a bull. Alderman Cunningham bridled and replied: "Tell Alderman Russell I am here, and if he wants to speak to me to come up here!"'

The outcome of this local battle for power was a win for Durham, with Ald. Cunningham being elected the first chairman of the new Committee. 'Being magnanimous, Andy Cunningham proposed Dr Russell as vice-chairman, which he accepted and honours were satisfied,' was how Jim remembered it.

This skirmish was only one example of the local power politics played out in the run-up to the formation of a Regional Committee and the building of a modern airport in Newcastle.

Although the North East now had the power base to establish a new airport it was to take another four years before the new terminal building was opened by the Prime Minister of the day, Harold Wilson. It would be unfair to blame local authorities for that delay; so many other factors were at work in deciding the best way forward.

When the Government announced the size of the grant, £100,000, there was some dismay; many people thought it should have been much more. One of them was Lord Hailsham who argued successfully for an increase. A Government grant was conditional on Whitehall approval of the appointment of consulting engineers and architects. J.D. looked back to that period and commented: 'On the Regional Airport Committee, in addition to Andy Cunningham as chairman, was T. Dan Smith, and hovering somewhere in the background was an architect called Poulson. So if the Government had not stipulated that they had a say in the appointment of consultants and architects, Mr Poulson could have finished up as architect to the new Newcastle Airport. I could have been involved quite innocently in the "Poulson Affair", but in fact I never was.'

The first major decision of the Regional Airport Committee was to appoint Frederick Snow and Partners as consulting engineers, and the firm of Yorke, Rosenburg and Mardall as architects, to advise on the development. Their final report was submitted in July, 1963 (only three months after their appointment) and provided a staged development for the new terminal complex. Construction work began in November, 1964 with the runway and new control building coming into operation in April, 1966, and the terminal complex a year later. The appointed consultants and architects also worked on the Gatwick Airport development, and the Newcastle terminal was loosely based on that plan.

The opening of a modern Newcastle Airport by the Prime Minister on 17 February 1967 marked the beginning of a new era of civil aviation for the North East region. An airport built to international standards presented an inviting introduction for businessmen and industrialists arriving to do business in the region. It stood as a jewel in the crown, linking the North East with Europe. The new complex, also featuring new passenger and air traffic control facilities, a new cargo area and enlarged car-parking area, drew admiring comments from passengers. The site of the new complex was to the north west of the old hangars, club house and runway, enabling the main runway to be lengthened, strengthened and regraded. It was increased in length to 2,332 metres though that major operation made Woolsington temporarily non-operational. In order not to interrupt airline services, J.D. came up with a novel idea: to transfer the whole of the Woolsington operation to RAF Ouston until the work was completed. The Air Ministry approved the switch, thus allowing civilian air transport to continue unimpeded. No one can deny that the idea of moving an airport was a bold one, especially during a North East winter. As it happened, the winter of 1965/66 turned out to be a vile and violent season which tested the Newcastle staff and crews to the limit.

Trouble began early when Woolsington crews arrived to set up air traffic control facilities in their Decca mobile radar caravan. Ouston, 200 feet higher than Woolsington above sea level, was being buffeted by gale-force winds. No sooner had the riggers got the caravan locked onto a base of wooden sleepers than a violent gust blew the caravan off its pedestal, though luckily the crew escaped injury. During the November of 1965 heavy snowfalls, coupled with high winds, forced Ouston to close down for nearly a week. The airline, BKS Air Transport operating Elizabethans and Dakotas, could neither get in or out of the airfield. That was despite valiant efforts by ground crews whose only snow-clearing equipment (shovels apart) was a down-thrust jet engine which was bolted down onto the back of a lorry and used for runway snow-clearing. Apart from the airfield shut-down, blizzards blocked the link road from the Military Road to Ouston for three days; staff became stranded on the airfield and could not reach home. Aside from those few hectic winter days, the temporary operation seems to have worked well.

The severe winter was not the only problem occupying the mind of Jim Denyer. His thoughts were constantly turning from Ouston to Woolsington where he began to fear that the new terminal complex might turn out to be too small, bearing in mind contractual delays and increased passenger traffic. J.D. takes up the story: 'One contractor went into liquidation at the same time as traffic was rapidly increasing. I began to have sleepless nights, fearing that the new airport would not cope. I discussed the matter with the consultants and as a result decided that the complex development should be advanced. I recommended to the Airport Committee that we should immediately progress to stage two of the development, they agreed and we pushed further ahead.' After 1967 and the opening of the new terminal complex, further improvements continued. As part of a staged development, the handling apron was enlarged to accommodate larger aircraft, and cargo handling was expanded, featuring new office accommodation for the increasing number of agents setting up in Newcastle. In addition, there was extensive expansion of the technical building housing air traffic control, flight/met. briefing and telecommunications.

THE GREAT TRANSPORT BATTLE: RAIL VERSUS AIR

As if running an international airport was not enough, Manager Denyer always had to keep a weather eye open for competition for his passengers. In fact the battle for supremacy on the Newcastle-London run between rail and air stayed with him for nearly forty years. And healthy competition had started before he ever arrived at Woolsington.

When Newcastle Municipal Airport opened for business in 1935, the main transport routes linking Tyneside with the rest of Britain were dominated by the railways. At that time, the country's rail net-work was divided into four areas and run by four different companies: the London and North Eastern; the London, Midland and Scottish, the Great Western; and the Southern Railway. Of those four, it could be argued that the LNER was the most efficient and prestigious company, well managed and possessing a Chief Engineer of outstanding talent—Sir Nigel Gresley.

It was the LNER Company that provided the strong opposition to any airline opening up a service from Newcastle to London. Even fifty years ago their crack express trains on the East Coast main line could cover the 270 miles to King's Cross in four hours. North East Airways, opening up the first Newcastle-London service in 1935 were unlucky to came up against the new A3 Pacific Locomotives, creating the Silver Jubilee and Silver Link Class, which were introduced the same year.

Those streamlined Silver Link locomotives, which pulled the luxury Pullman coaches of the *Flying Scotsman* could depart from King's Cross at 10 a.m. and arrive at Newcastle Central Station at 2 p.m. On sections of the track, these engines were achieving speeds of 100 m.p.h. before the Second World War, though it has to be said that the ordinary steam trains, stopping at main line stations *en route* took much longer involving sometimes journeys of six hours to London from Tyneside.

That was the kind of formidable competition that the early airlines at

Woolsington had to come to terms with. North East Airways, which inaugurated services from Newcastle to London after 1935 countered with the slogan: 'FLY TO LONDON IN 2$^{1}/_{2}$ HOURS!'

The 'Big Four' railway companies, LNER, LMS, GWR and SR then executed a deft business move by joining with Imperial Airways to form 'Railway Air Services', a consortium that launched intercity UK services linking one part of the country with another.

Now the railway companies had covered themselves with 'double indemnity' against other airline competition and could afford to launch a new advertising campaign which dangled the carrot of travelling in luxury on trains like the Pullman. The attractions included a 'Louis XVl Restaurant, services of a hairdresser and a ladies retirement room with attendants'. Further, Sir Nigel Gresley stepped up the speeds of his Pacific locomotives, achieving a world speed record for a steam train in 1938 when his *Mallard* Pacific attained a speed of 126 mph on the East Coast main line.

During the first decade of Jim Denyer's reign at Newcastle, airlines stepped up their services to London and British Railways had to look to their laurels. By the end of the l950s, flying first Dakotas and then Elizabethans, the BKS Air Transport Company had reduced the journey time into Northolt, Bovington, by half. The average flight time from Newcastle to Northolt, and later Heathrow was one hour and twenty minutes.

As the airport manager recalled: 'Now local industrialists and businessmen began to desert British Rail in droves, particularly those travellers going on to Europe and foreign centres from Heathrow. British Rail reacted by introducing faster trains in the sixties and seventies, employing aggressive advertising with slogans like, 'FLY TO LONDON BY RAIL!' Businessmen were attracted to the air by the ease of flying down to London on the early flight, attending business meetings through the day and returning home the same night. By the end of the 1960s, the jet airliners on the Newcastle-to-London run, with a flight time of only fifty minutes, threw down a new challenge to British Rail. Depending on wind conditions on the day, that flight time was often beaten. Unbelievably, the record flight time from take-off at Heathrow to touch down at Newcastle is only twenty-six minutes. J.D. recalled: 'The pilot that day was Capt. Larry Miller whom we taught to fly at Newcastle. A strong tail wind upped his speed through the air to over 600 m.p.h.—the stewardesses hardly had time to serve a cup of tea!'

British Rail's retort was to come up with an attractive package for local businessmen travelling to London. Their 'Executive' package included first-class travel and full English breakfast going down (and newspapers); car and Underground tickets in the capital; and late dinner on the return journey. Even so, British Airways continued to increase their passenger traffic; by the end of the 1980s they were carrying more than 350,000 passengers per year in their pure jet airliners. This fierce competition between rail and air has continued up to the present day. J.D. remembered that despite the battle for passengers, Newcastle Airport and local British Rail had a good working relationship. For example, if a major carrier was unexpectedly diverted to Woolsington by bad weather, BR would either hold trains for airline passengers or sometimes put on special trains to enable them to complete their journey to the capital.

By 1991 British Rail had upped the stakes in the fight for passengers by opening the new, fast electrified East Coast main line network, which slashed journey time from Newcastle to Kings Cross. During that same year, Newcastle International Airport hit the headlines with the opening of its new Metro Rail link into the heart of Newcastle Central Station effectively linking the airport to the national railway system. It got off to a flying start with some 10,000 people taking the Metro from the centre of the city to spend the day at the airport. The Tyne and Wear Passenger Transport Executive met the cost of building the Metro Rail, some £12m., with additional funds from the Airport Authority and the EEC.

# Chapter IX

## THE ANATOMY OF AN AIRPORT

## A DAY IN THE LIFE OF AN AIRPORT MANAGER

The unpredictable and often hectic working day for James H. Denyer, Director of Newcastle International Airport began when he backed his car out of the garage of his Ponteland home and switched his car radio to the frequency of Air Traffic Control. Listening in to ground-to-air radio intelligence, he learned about any important incident as it happened. So by the time he entered the approaches to the airfield he was ready to act. Waiting to update him as he walked through the entrance of the terminal building was the duty officer. Although it was the start of another long day, Jim Denyer and his staff were already buzzing with renewed vigour to ensure the efficient handling of passengers, and the safe passage of airliners in and out of Newcastle. If all was well, he began his morning rounds.

First came a call at the Information Desk to ask about any late flights or hold ups; then a walk round the whole of the concourse to check on its cleanliness and the conditions that day; then a chat with one or two local businessmen, arriving to either fly down to London or into the heart of Europe. 'That was a good time to elicit from them if they had any complaints, or any suggestions to make regarding check-in procedures'. Only then did he enter his own office, where his first action was to switch on his desk ground-to-air radio to listen to the intelligence and directions going through the ether to aeroplanes in the Newcastle zone. That was followed by a run down of the diary of events of the day with his secretary, before he started 'flying' his own desk, and dealing with problems as they developed.

That was the attraction of the job of airport boss—no two days were alike; there was no set routine, J.D. had to be ready for any emergency. If there was no operational problem, he might be faced with an industrial relations row (though at Newcastle there were very few), or he might have to deal with a serious complaint from a passenger. If and when trouble was brewing, he always said that 'the buck stops here.' Treated with respect, and even affection by staff at the airport, he nevertheless could fight his corner; and when necessary, could 'tear a strip' off anyone, though the record shows that Newcastle Airport was so well run that a great row was an exception to the rule. As Jim put it: 'Over the years, I always said to my staff that my door was open daily, and if they had any problems they shouldn't hesitate to bring them to me. In that way, potential trouble could often be averted.'

He was well-known for defending his staff against anyone if he thought they had a case. One of the main reasons for the success of this sharp-eyed man, little in stature but big in everything else, was his ability to handle people from all walks of life, from a Dinnington miner to a visiting Royal. What he didn't tell people was that years ago, during his service in the Royal Air Force, he had studied psychology and had spent time on a man-management course. As a RAF Flight Lieutenant, during war and peace, he had had plenty of experience in handling personnel; and just as he had been a fighter during war, he became a strong leader in times of peace. The great challenge arriving on his desk at Woolsington was meat and drink to him. One slogan which he collected years ago was: 'The difficult we can do immediately; the impossible takes a little longer!'

During his busy day, he always found time to talk to his directors of operations and finance. His policy was to delegate where he could, but to keep in touch with all his staff. Large, long lunches were not on his menu; he preferred sandwiches and tea at his desk, enabling him to discuss happenings of the day with his personal assistant.

If the office of the Director of the Airport was the administrative driving force, the 'nerve centre' of the operational side was Air Traffic Control. This is recognised to be the most stressful job, in which mistakes cannot be contemplated. Because of the high volume of traffic handled, no international airport could operate without a first-class air traffic control system, which is split between the Visual Control (top of the ATC tower) and Radar Control (at the bottom). The operation is carried out by ATCOs (Air Traffic Controllers) who are often assisted by ATCAs (Air Traffic Control Assistants). Visual Control duties include directing aircraft on runways, taxi-ways and aprons and controlling any vehicles which have reason to traverse the air-side. The duties of Radar Control include giving directions to pilots of incoming aircraft, including speed, height and direction, right up to final approach. In addition to the above, international airports provide an Instrument Landing System service for approaching aircraft, this ILS, making for faultless landings, allows the pilot to land manually or on automatic landing. Newcastle operates a Category 2 system.

Newcastle International Airport has equipped its ATC with the most modern equipment money can buy to handle this hair-trigger operation. The radar system can target up to one hundred tracks over sixty miles at heights of up to 60,000 feet. In practice, the duty ATCO is more likely to be dealing with some dozen aircraft tracks which represent aircraft flying in the Newcastle operational area.

Although working in Air Traffic Control is a stressful occupation, it is the antithesis of the celluloid image portrayed in American aircraft disaster movies by Hollywood film directors. Instead of frenzied chain-smoking actors shouting out instructions across the tower, the real thing is a cathedral-like calm with ATCOs going about their business with a quiet efficiency and total concentration. As with landings, ATC is also responsible for the safe and expeditious flow of take-offs.

J.D. underlined the importance of the ATC at any airport. 'Air Traffic Control is of paramount importance in the operation of an airport; it has a stress factor which is limited by law—a controller can only operate for a short period of time (sometimes only ninety minutes) without a break, depending on the volume of traffic at the time. If he loses concentration, the result can be extremely serious.'

Few people outside aviation circles know that controllers, just like airline crews, have to undergo rigorous medical checks annually. Failure to pass can result in the loss of licence and job. It is not surprising, therefore, to find that air traffic controllers have their own special insurance scheme. Thousands of aircraft are guided in and out of Woolsington every year, and it is a credit to the ATC operation that no major disaster has ever happened. In more than fifty years of operation, that record speaks for itself. At Newcastle there are over 60,000 aircraft movements a year.

However, it would be misleading to say that Newcastle did not have its fair share of incidents and emergencies. Older staff have not forgotten the Comet crash of the seventies. A beautiful Comet jet airliner, flying a training schedule came into land without the undercarriage lowered and in place. Although it made a good landing in the circumstances it was badly damaged and declared a write off. Fortunately, none of the crew of seven were hurt.

In addition to its civilian role, Newcastle Airport is a master diversion airfield for the RAF and NATO aircraft. Often these Service planes arrive at very short notice and are periodically caught up in some kind of emergency. Sometimes RAF jet aircraft make 'bird strikes' forcing them to make emergency landings. The North East coast, a habitat for countless numbers of sea birds, is part of the training ground for low-flying RAF planes; jet engines striking sea birds spells trouble. There have been other incidents involving military aircraft, like the time an American A-10 Tankbuster lost an engine and made for Woolsington. Making an emergency landing, it used all but fifty metres of the air strip before it could be brought to a halt.

One testing period of the year for Air Traffic Control has nothing to do with military aircraft; it might be called 'the package holiday pressure cooker'. The all-inclusive holiday to sun-drenched resorts has been the bread-and-butter big earner for Newcastle for years. When this traffic peaks in summer it can test the nerve-ends of most people working at the airport. Woolsington is part of a vast European network of airports feeding aircraft into an 'airliner funnel' over France, which is the aviation stepping-off place for resorts like Majorca and Spain. Every seasoned traveller at this time will have his or her own story of hold-ups and the fact is that aircraft are crammed like sardines into this French 'funnel' and there is little margin for error. A technical hold-up to a holiday charter aircraft flying from Newcastle of, say, only ten or fifteen minutes could cause it to lose its place in the queue resulting in delays of hours. In the last few years the situation has improved, much to the relief of pilots and passengers, though hold ups still occur sometimes at peak periods.

An essential part of Air Traffic Control is ATC Engineering which, up to a few years ago, was known as the Telecommunications Section. Newcastle Airport could not operate safely and efficiently without fully serviced sophisticated apparatus which is the responsibility of the Woolsington 'boffins'. These backroom boys may never be seen by passengers but they are a vital cog in maintaining the heartbeat of the airport operation.

The vigilance of airport security is of course of paramount importance. In the 1990s there can be no relaxing at any airport in the war against drug traffickers, hi-jackers and terrorists, not to mention the attempted smuggling of other goods which goes on all the time at Britain's airports.

When Jim Denyer managed Newcastle Airport he saw to it that there was never any relaxation in the security of the operation. There is a triumvirate of security at Newcastle which work together as a tightly-knit unit. Working with the airport private Police Force are specially trained firemen who have a responsibility for the safety of aircraft and passengers in times of emergency.

The third member of this group is HM Customs who bear a special responsibility in the battle against drug smugglers and law-breakers. The record shows that although the North East is not the drug capital of England, gangs have, from time to time, plotted to flood northern cities with drugs like heroin and cocaine. In fact, during 1982, after a cutback in Customs Officers working in the region, the Newcastle Customs Branch of the Civil and Public Servants Union stated publicly: 'Heroin and other drugs have never before been so freely available on the streets of the North East'. The pressure on Customs and Immigration Officers can often be intense, especially during peak seasons when the flow of passengers doubles, and passenger traffic at Newcastle is increasing all the time. Whereas a third of a million passengers were handled at Newcastle in 1982, the figure has risen to more than one and a half million in 1992. That requires all services connected with passenger arrivals and departures to remain vigilant at all times. The officers of HM Immigration and Customs are primed to stop unlawful entry and any breaches of official allowances by passengers arriving from abroad.

Whenever J.D. talked about the Police Force at Newcastle Airport there was a gleam of pride in his eyes—he remembered the days when airport security was an elderly night watchman and his small Yorkshire terrier! Since 1952, security has been tightened out of all recognition. When the new terminal building was opened in 1967, J.D. introduced 'Denyer's Dogs' into the security operation. 'I have always maintained that a policeman working with a dog is worth more than two policemen' he said. The dogs, German shepherds, live in style in purpose built kennels known among staff as 'The Doggie Hilton'. Newcastle was the first municipal airport in the country to introduce dogs and remains the only municipal airport to use them today.

Although the size of the Police Force at Woolsington is kept secret for security reasons, there are always enough men in uniform to check over passengers, and keep a tight hold on safety and security. Policemen and policewomen operate sophisticated X-ray and other modern detection equipment which can now pinpoint explosive material in luggage. In addition, archway metal detectors are used in the search for firearms and other weapons. The airport police, in uniform approved by Northumbria Police, while not possessing the powers of the Civil constabulary, are empowered to enforce the by-laws of Newcastle Airport. Those powers include searching passengers' luggage before departure (and if necessary on arrival) as well as carrying out security patrols throughout the airport complex.

Newcastle is particularly proud of its fire-fighting service; it is second to none. Some years ago, the Civil Aviation Authority asked Newcastle to assist with the training of firemen from third world countries, a request that speaks for itself. According to J.D. 'Although the travelling public may rarely see them, the fire-fighters are in the forefront of the operation, first into action when an emergency occurs.' The majority of firemen at Newcastle hold Certificates of Competency issued by the Civil Aviation Authority. In the event of a crash or other accidents involving aeroplanes, firemen can turn on more than 40,000 gallons of foam, forming a 'blanket of survival' in less than two minutes. The Newcastle fleet includes superfast fire tenders and a powerful 'travelling tool box' carrying power tools which can saw through an aircraft in a matter of seconds. The fleet, which may be called into action in any part of the airfield or its environs, is self sufficient, carrying generators and its own high-powered lighting. By 1992 airport firemen were operating from a new air-side station complete with tower.

FLYING THE FREIGHT AND MOVING THE MAIL

The first commercial contract to carry the Royal Mail by air was signed as long ago as the 1930s. By 1939, North Eastern Airways were flying the post in de Havilland Rapide bi-planes between Newcastle and London. In more recent years, an aircraft carrying thousands of letters has left Newcastle nightly for a network rendezvous at Liverpool, where it has collected mail for delivery on North East doorsteps the next morning. In addition, daily data post and mail flights were undertaken to Manchester.

By 1992, the Post Office was able to announce the creation of a new, super air network for the speedier carrying of mail round the country. The Royal Mail Skynet flights enable millions more letters per year to drop onto the nation's doormats the day after posting. Gill Air, based at Newcastle, has successfully tendered to fly the Skynet service using two aircraft between Woolsington and Stansted, and another two operating between Belfast and the West Country. Gill's success will mean long-term job security for up to 130 staff nationwide with ninety based at Newcastle.

When it comes to cargo-carrying, Newcastle was rather slower off the ground. The freight business did not take off until after the last war with Ulster Aviation a pioneer, flying between Tyneside and Northern Ireland. The quaint, chopped off single-wing aircraft, suitably called the Aerovan carried among other cargo, radio sets manufactured on the Team Valley Trading Estate.

For various operational and economic reasons, freight-carrying was slow to gather momentum. By the early sixties, the airport was only handling fourteen tons of freight a week; shipments were carried in the small baggage holds of Dakotas and Elizabethans. During the 1970s, with the introduction of jet aircraft, Newcastle set about the business of winning the market to centres like Amsterdam, Oslo, Bergen, Stavanger, Paris and Dublin. According to J.D. 'In the 1950s and 1960s North East industrialists shied away from air-freighting because of the cost compared with road and rail.' Today the bulk of air cargo is containerised and transferred by road overnight to the London airports for onward air transportation by the big jets. However, that is only the bulk cargo side of the business. In addition, thousands of smaller items of cargo are carried regularly on scheduled services, to home and foreign airports. 'Cargo-carrying is growing fast at Newcastle' according to J.D. 'As the North East has come through recessions better than most, more industries have been established and so the freight business goes up.' One of the latest developments planned is to establish a 'cargo village' at Newcastle, due to be completed in 1993, injecting a new dynamic into the operation at Woolsington: national and international freight-only operators, flying giant cargo-jets could be operating from the airport in the future.

Something that J.D. discovered over the years was that if there was any trouble with cargo, it usually concerned animals, as in the case of the missing greyhound. On one particular day, a cargo from Dublin included a valuable greyhound, which had made the journey without incident, travelling in a padded wooden crate. The trouble began after the greyhound had disembarked and was placed in its crate on a flat wagon behind a towing vehicle. *En route* to the cargo shed, the towing vehicle had cause to brake suddenly, and the crate was thrown against the back of the cab, bursting it open. The released greyhound ran off like greased lightning in the direction of Dinnington. Hotly pursued by the ground crew, the speedy animal left them standing and vanished out of sight, never to be seen again. There were one or two red faces at Woolsington that night when the charter company had to telephone the new owner, apologise, and obtain the greyhound's value so that a claim could be made with the insurance company.

Another incident related to the 'Hamster Invasion of Woolsington'. When fog closed down London airfields one night, a British Airways 747, flying in from Chicago, was diverted to Newcastle. After the Jumbo touched down and the rear hold was opened the ground staff rubbed their eyes in disbelief for the hold was teeming with rodents. J.D. remembers one of the ground crew shouting: 'This bloody aircraft is crawling with rats!' Jim continues the story: 'In fact they were not rats but hamsters. I went to have a look and they were running round all over the place. I checked the manifest to discover that 750 hamsters had been loaded in boxes in Chicago. In fact hamsters in three boxes had gnawed through the wire and escaped. We rounded up what we could but in the end, more than fifty were still missing. Some had hidden in the large aircraft hold. We couldn't find them.' This unusual cargo presented a headache for British Airways manager, Jim Shields, who was detained at the airport for hours trying to establish—with the help of police and health officers—whether any hamsters had escaped into the airport complex. Pressed by the officers, Jim Shields came out with the rejoinder: 'Have a good look round the apron. If you find any hamsters and they squeak with a American accent, you'll know they're not ours!' J.D. 's postscript: 'I don't think that went down very well with the police and health officers, though it raised a laugh among staff.'

Looking back on the battle to win freight business for Newcastle, it took until the 1980s before the business finally took off. In 1986, staff handled 3,900 tons of cargo, a figure that had jumped to 5,800 tons by 1989 and which has continued to increase.

By 1992, more than a dozen different air freight agencies were operating from Newcastle, an indication that all freight records were to be broken in the future.

THE PASSENGERS' VIEW OF THE AIRPORT

It seems a little odd that in the township of an international airport, pulsating with a wide variety of aviation services, the airline passenger's only real conversation will be with the girl behind the check-in desk.

During 1982 passengers at Newcastle were introduced to the more efficient island desk system, making check-in easier and quicker. In fact check-in desks at Woolsington were manned by three different handling agents. Dan-Air was taken over in 1992, leaving Servisair and North East Aviation Services. Dan-Air, associated with Newcastle for many years, had a basic staff of some thirty people, rising to more than forty in the busy holiday season (see postscript). Servisair, which began operations at Newcastle in 1968, handles hundreds of thousands of passengers every year, including many package holiday clients. North East Aviation Services, a more recent handling agent, was formed by former staff of British Airways who were granted the franchise to handle BA's contract, and were also in the market for other new business, running a twenty-four-hour operation.

Coupled with the speed of check-in facilities is the swift and safe handling of passengers' luggage which, as J.D. said, is of 'paramount importance'. Passengers need peace of mind that there will be no mishap with their baggage.

On the other hand, when passengers disembark from large jets at Newcastle at the end of a long journey they do not wish to be delayed by slow baggage handling. At Newcastle they are fortunate. As soon as an aircraft lands, cargo holds are thrown open, luggage is transferred to trucks which whisk them onto the start of the conveyor moving chain, which ends in either carousel or 'race track' baggage reclamation units. At Newcastle, travellers' luggage frequently arrives in the terminal building before the passengers do. In addition, ground staff man all types of equipment necessary to service a modern jet. When it comes to looking after disabled passengers, Newcastle is one of the best equipped airports in the country.

The catering facilities at Woolsington today are a far cry from the primitive refreshments available to passengers in the 1950s, when the single teaspoon was nailed to the counter with string, and the pinnacle of the service was tea, or coffee and biscuits. In the 1990s, Newcastle's facilities rival those of any municipal airport in the country. In addition to the Hadrian Restaurant there is an extensive buffet and an attractive bar area. There is also a bar and buffet in the international departure lounge, as well as the travellers' friend, the duty-free shop. J.D. explained:'The Airport Authority does not have the expertise to run the duty-free operation which is let out to a concessionaire. The practice of bulk-buying by airports allows the passenger to buy cheaply, and the concessionaire and the airport to profit. There are many thousands of pounds to be made from the sale of duty-free goods and the airport is fearful of the threat to introduce new legislation which will abolish duty-free shops within the Common Market. That would result in higher charges to the airlines which would be passed on to passengers.'

# KEEPING AN AIRPORT GOING

The seventy-strong engineering staff at Newcastle—which has the responsibility of maintaining a 540-acre site with buildings, runways and aprons—did not exist when J.D. was appointed Commandant in 1952. Today the Engineering Department has two major roles: operation and maintenance, planning and development. Forty years ago, with no engineering section stationed on the airfield, Newcastle Corporation Engineers carried out airport work when it could be fitted in. Often maintenance work took place at weekends which cost the airport budget dearly with double-time payments. When Newcastle Corporation surrendered management of the airport to the North East Regional Committee, J.D. created his own Engineering Department to coincide with the opening of the new terminal in 1967. J.D. looked back: 'That was one of the best things I did in the 1960s. At a stroke we could start work on lighting, heating, emergency power, motor transport maintenance and various other jobs. Few people realised the extent of the duties which fell on the engineering side. For example, today more than one hundred vehicles have to be maintained including fire tender, electrically powered vehicles and snow-clearing vehicles.'

Newcastle's outstanding runway lighting system has also to be maintained, and during 1992 finishing touches were being put to a new fire station, strategically situated overlooking the main runway. The airport engineering department may not often be in the news, though without its key personnel the airport operation would quickly grind to a halt.

To demonstrate the cost of engineering operations, the airport's bill is more than £2,000 every time the runway is de-iced. On the other hand, airport engineering saves the airport thousands of pounds by employing its extensive technical and scientific skills on new in-house developments. The installation of touch-down zones and additional arch lighting for the modern instrument runway lighting system is a good example. Perhaps not quite so scientific, but nevertheless a pleasing example of in-house skills was the construction of sophisticated teak furniture for the new terminal roof feature. J.D. points out this example as a money-saver. 'When the contractors demolished the outside staircase to make way for the new terminal building they piled the teak stair-treads to one side for burning. I was aware that this was valuable timber which could be put to good use which prompted me to have it removed to the joinery. Later it left that workshop to re-appear as attractive teak furniture for the benefit of the public.'

## THE ROLE OF NORTH EAST LOCAL AUTHORITIES

A paramount factor in the success of Newcastle International Airport has been the system of co-operation between local authorities who own the airport, and the management system at the sharp end. So successful has the arrangement been that a Government Minister is on record as saying that Newcastle is an example to many other local authority-owned airports in the country.

Jim Denyer had the rare distinction of being one of the few airport managers who had worked for three different kinds of local authorities. When he arrived in 1952 he worked for Newcastle Corporation through the Municipal Airport Committee. In 1963 his employers changed to the North East Municipal Airport Committee. When he retired in 1989, Newcastle International Airport Ltd had taken over. Today's authority is a private limited company with the total share capital held by North East local authorities: Newcastle City, the Metropolitan Borough Councils of Sunderland, Gateshead, North Tyneside and South Tyneside, and the County Councils of Northumberland and Durham.

The team at the top has generally consisted of more than twenty elected councillors (representing the respective authorities) plus the Airport Managing Director and his two Directors. It is a credit to the region that such a large body of mixed councillors and managers have been able to produce an efficient and far-sighted team.

It should be recorded that the management strategy was spelled out clearly from the start, as J.D. remembers. 'At the first meeting of the North East Regional Airport Committee in 1963 I told the councillors: You don't know the sharp end from the blunt end of an airport, that is my job. If there are going to be any bouquets for the airport in the future, they are yours. If there are any brick-bats, they are mine. But I assure you the brick-bats will be minimal.' J.D. continued: 'The councillors laughed and it went down well with the Committee. They did not interfere with the day-to-day running of the airport; I cannot remember the Committee ever turning down a recommendation from me that would enhance the airport's future.'

When J.D. arrived to manage the Woolsington operation in 1952, the airport was costing Newcastle tax-payers thousands of pounds every year. During the Denyer dynasty, and particularly after the formation of the Regional Airport Committee, the airport forged ahead. For years now it has returned a handsome trading profit.

# Chapter X

## INTO THE SEVENTIES—A MOMENTOUS DECADE

## THE JET AGE ARRIVES—HOLIDAYS ABROAD FOR ALL

By 1972 James Henry Denyer had completed twenty years service as the chief executive at Woolsington, and was known far and wide as 'Mr Newcastle Airport'. This was a sobriquet given him by the Press, though after two decades of progress and having pushed Woolsington to the forefront of the country's municipal airports, it was not undeserved. His dynamic leadership, coupled with a tenacity that would not allow him to come off second best—no matter how high the authority—gained him respect among the many people by now employed at Newcastle Airport. At this period of his career one member of his staff remarked, 'He's got a huge ego for a little guy but his keenness is tremendous.' Another commented, 'If he thought that he was in the right he would yield to no one; he's fair above everything else.'

No one could argue that J.D. did not make the airport his life. The hallmark of his career was tireless grafting built on an appetite for work. His zest for his job was such that his wife, Mary, once joked with him: 'As you're married to the airport, why don't you complete the partnership and move your bed there!' For Jim Denyer the airport never shut! His home telephone was never off the hook. During the formative years of the airport's development, he could not plan even his annual holiday. If things were going well at Woolsington, he would suddenly inform the family: 'Right, we're off on holiday in a couple of day's time.' While that might have a put a strain on pre-planning for Mrs Denyer, it was an exciting time to live through.

After twenty years at the top, Jim knew a thing or two about airport management. Asked once to list the attributes required to run an international airport he came up with the following: to possess the patience of Job, the memory of an elephant, the power of psychology, the art of negotiation, a wide knowledge of local and national politics, the ability to mix and talk to people, the flair to work smoothly with all airlines and anticipate their demands, to have first-class contacts, and to possess the skin of a rhinoceros! Not that he needed all those to herald in the new age of the jet airliner in the early 1970s, though the more powerful aircraft now using Newcastle created a new problem—the shattering roar of the jet planes taking off and coming in to land had local residents complaining in their droves. According to J.D. 'they complained of broken sleep and said their television viewing was rudely interrupted by the noise of jet engines overhead. Complaints came in by letter, by telephone and some were made in person. Most of the complaints came from residents to the north and west of Newcastle; in the end I became inured to abuse from complainants.'

As time went on and the argument that the new noisier planes would considerably shorten journeys struck home, the groundswell of complaint subsided. The previous 'carping crowd' were only too pleased to step into one of the new jet aircraft and speed away on a package holiday to a sunspot abroad!

The new phenomenon of vacation-taking—the fully inclusive holiday abroad—took off in the 1970s. At the beginning of that decade, domestic services were still busier than international services, though by 1973, international services from Newcastle, mainly package holiday traffic, had caught up. For the remainder of the decade they became a big money earner for the airport.

At the start of the seventies, some 400,000 passengers were carried per year to and from Newcastle; by 1980 that number had more than doubled to over 1,000,000. The lion's share of the increase was due to the expansion of package holidays. J.D. was now aware of a Geordie social phenomenon: whether the region's economy was in boom or bust, he would take his holiday abroad at any price. That idiosyncrasy knocks on the head the economic argument that in times of recession luxuries like foreign holidays are abandoned. J.D. put it this way: 'The Geordie, since I got to know him, has always given his holiday priority, even over buying a new car or a new television receiver.'

As the demand for package holidays increased, there was a great need for national tour operators to set up in Newcastle and fly local holiday-makers direct to sunspots abroad. J.D. launched a powerful campaign to this end, but it took personal visits to London and Luton to bring the big operators like Thomson and Inter-Sun to Woolsington. On occasions he had to dangle a carrot in front of the operators and the airlines to move up from the South. It could be a concession such as fifty per cent reduction in landing fees on new routes, though that concession ended as soon as the operator broke even.

At the end of the day, J.D. got what he wanted for Newcastle; operators like Thomson, Horizon, Global, Wings, Ellerman-Sunlight and Air Tours became household names there. Sometimes, when big holiday business was pulsating through the Newcastle terminal, J.D. would be reminded by an old photograph of the holiday air service of the fifties. In the early fifties handfuls of local holiday-makers flew in second-hand, thirty-seater Dakota aircraft to 'faraway places' like the Isle of Man, Jersey and Guernsey! A new horizon opened up at the end of that decade when the Euravia airline company introduced Super Constellation four-engine aircraft for transportation of holiday-makers from Newcastle to Spain and the Balearics. Later, the Thomson Organisation bought out Euravia and renamed the airline, 'Britannia Airways' after the type of plane they were flying. The arrival of Sky Tours at Woolsington was a dream come true for the Geordie holiday-maker who wanted an 'all-in' vacation abroad.

Subsequently, Thomson Holidays became Britain's number one tour operator, modernising their Britannia fleet with the new Boeing 737s. Another early operator on the holiday scene was Dan-Air, flying passengers from Newcastle to Norway by the 1960s. The explosion of the package holiday trade from Woolsington continued into the eighties and nineties.

All the news was not good news. Information reached the airport director that the Conservative Government was planning a major reorganisation of local government in 1974. The alarm bells rang when J.D. discovered that the new Tyne and Wear Metropolitan County Council would include the district parishes of Woolsington and Dinnington, while Northumberland County would include the parish of Ponteland. That would result in Newcastle administering the former, and Castle Morpeth the latter, creating a headache for the airport manager.

Denyer recalls: 'This chaotic arrangement of splitting the airport in two was to result in complex administrative arrangements, particularly where local authority services were concerned. I contacted the planners in the Department of the Environment who were unaware that they had split the airport down the middle. Despite my complaint, Whitehall did absolutely nothing.'

When the 1974 Act received the Royal Assent and became law, the airport director's worst fears were realised. Aircraft stands numbers 4, 5, 6 and half of 7 fell in Tyne and Wear (Newcastle) while stands 1, 2, 3, 8, 9, 10 and 11 fell in Northumberland County (Castle Morpeth). The terminal building also fell in the latter. All that raised several problems: for example, which authority would provide back-up fire services during an airport emergency? 'One person made the silly suggestion that where aircraft came to a standstill at the airport determined which authority should be involved! Instead, it was agreed that in case of fire, the Gosforth Station of the Tyne and Wear Fire Brigade, the nearest, would act as a back-up fire service.'

There was also a mix-up relating to the collection of refuse from the airport. Newcastle refuse collectors would not cross the line into the Castle Morpeth area and take rubbish from the terminal. Conversely, the refuse collectors from Castle Morpeth would not take it from the Newcastle side of the line. The airport manager was faced with the prospect of paying two authorities for collecting rubbish from the airport! When giving after-dinner speeches J.D. used to joke that he played one authority off against another and paid neither for refuse collection! Up to the date of his retirement in 1989, the airport was still 'split down the middle' though the Boundary Commission was reviewing the situation following the demise of the Tyne and Wear County Council. The stakes were high as the airport environs and terminal building areas are a large rateable asset to any authority.

This Whitehall gaffe which took the 'body' of Newcastle Airport apart was to have repercussions for years to come. Not least in the visit of an American President in 1977, which gave rise to the biggest security operation Tyneside has ever witnessed. Weeks before Jimmy Carter (then USA President) was due to arrive, J.D. was visited by an Army Colonel from the American Embassy in London. He informed the airport manager that the CIA, the FBI and White House Security Staff wanted to discuss the forthcoming visit. Unperturbed, J.D. told the Colonel that they had better all come to see him together

When the day of the visit arrived, the Americans certainly made a strong impression on the staff at Woolsington. Six security 'heavies' accompanied the Colonel into J.D.'s office. The airport manager picked up the story: 'There were two Secret Service men from each of the departments; they were of impressive stature, wearing fawn or white raincoats with 'bulges' just visible under the left arm-pits.

'When the discussion got under way, I was astounded that each of the three services was intent on making their own pitch, each reluctant to yield to the others on points of security. They were talking at cross purposes about the President's visit and I was conscious that we were getting nowhere. I had to do something, so suddenly I thumped hard on my desk top and shouted "Stop!" There was a deathly hush. I informed the group that Air Force One (The President's plane) would be given permission to land when I was satisfied with the security status of the airport. I would be happy to consider their advice and co-operate but I would make the final decision. Their mouths dropped open momentarily, but the trick seemed to have worked.

'After further discussion, they thanked me for my co-operation and said that they would keep me in the picture and left. After they had gone the Colonel remained behind to say: "I have been with those security men all over the world and I have never seen them spoken to like that!" I replied, "My God, if anything goes wrong my head will be on the chopping block!"'

Everyone remembers the success of the Jimmy Carter visit, his famous 'Howay the Lads' riposte to the large crowds in Newcastle and his cementing of the presidential bond with the North East region with his visit to Washington Old Hall, the ancestral home of George Washington. The President's visit went off extremely well, Carter being mobbed by great enthusiastic crowds. When it was all over and the President returned to

Woolsington to join his aircraft, his security men, including the CIA, warmly thanked J.D. for efficient arrangements at the airport.

After the President returned to the United States, he sent J.D. a signed Certificate of Appreciation and invited him to visit his home town of Plains. Following the Presidential visit, and in recognition of Jim Denyer's contribution to national aviation over the years, he was awarded the OBE. At that time he had served on the Air Transport and Travel Industry Training Board for eleven years.

When it was all over, J.D. did hear about one complaint. When Carter's Air Force One arrived at Woolsington it taxied into stand No. 2 at the airport, and that lay within the Castle Morpeth Council District. The Mayor of Castle Morpeth was understandably miffed when he was not invited to form part of the VIP welcoming party; he made a complaint arguing that protocol demanded a presence.

Following Jimmy Carter, the next VIP scheduled to visit Woolsington was the Queen Mother. That prompted a pre-visit to the airport from the Lord Lieutenant to check arrangements. He requested that the Royal aircraft should be parked in the Newcastle segment of the airport. J.D. told him that the Queen Mother liked to be near the public so that she could wave to people on the terminal roof which would give him a problem if the plane was parked there: 'With a wry smile, I informed the Lord Lieut. that the only aircraft stand we could use that day was Stand Number 7 and though the nose of the plane would be in Castle Morpeth, the aircraft exit would be in the Newcastle Authority area…Although that was said in jest, it was taken seriously so I agreed that the plane should be parked in that spot, and all went well!'

The fifties had been a busy time for J.D. in more ways than one. After the staging of the national air races, a premier event on the aviation calendar, he had had to promote a publicity campaign to put Newcastle on the map. He succeeded beyond his wildest dreams. Following his outstanding air racing days, the sixties and seventies witnessed Newcastle Airport grow in stature. In the early seventies, the Aero Club hosted an international Air Rally which attracted pre-eminent pilots from all over Europe. They came to Woolsington from France, Germany, Belgium and other parts of Europe to compete in spot-landings, navigation competitions and other events held over Northumberland. J.D. summed it up: 'It gave our foreign friends a good impression of the North East of England, presenting a rather different picture to the way we were portrayed in the national Press.'

The more affluent society of the sixties, and the emergence of Spain as the sunspot of Europe that exploded passenger traffic from Newcastle, continued at a pace during the seventies. The total number of passengers handled in 1960 was some 119,000. By 1970 that number had more than doubled to 416,000 and was rising fast. The challenge of rapid expansion had landed on Jim Denyer's desk with a thump. He had already forewarned the North East Regional Airport Committee about new pressures on airport handling and the need for further expansion. The Committee had called for an overall development plan for the next twenty years from Sir Frederick Snow and Partners.

By 1971, the Airport Authority had begun a new expansion programme which included an extension of the handling apron by some forty per cent, the construction of an additional cargo stand and the development of a general aviation apron. The planned next stage was to build a parallel taxi-way but, incredibly, it took nearly another twenty years to complete much to the chagrin of the airport manager. There was also a plan to extend the runway to 9,500 feet to cater for the growing intercontinental group charter and inclusive tour holiday market.

This question of runway length was to bother Jim Denyer for some years to come. The facts are that Newcastle possesses one good runway which was put down more than twenty years ago, constructed to a minimum thickness of thirty inches with an additional asphalt wearing surface, accepting a high loading factor. The runway is 2,332 metres long and forty-six metres wide. By comparison, the main runway of Manchester Ringway Airport is 3,050 metres long. Newcastle's limitations were to restrict the biggest, wide-bodied jet aircraft using Newcastle. By law a Jumbo Jet Boeing 747 could not leave Newcastle with a full load of passengers, luggage and cargo. From Newcastle, it would leave without cargo but with full load of passengers and luggage, with sufficient fuel to arrive at their first destination point, for example Toronto or New York. Aviation law states that an aircraft has to have the capability of losing an engine on reaching V1 (velocity 1, the rotation for take off) and being able to pull up in the available distance of the runway. That safety factor is related mainly to total weight of loaded aircraft and length of runway, so that Jumbo Jets can use Newcastle with the cargo limit proviso.

The airport manager carried out feasibility studies for extending the runway, a major project costing much money to implement. One problem was that one section of the busy road bordering the Dinnington side of the airfield would have to be closed. Throughout the seventies this question of lengthening the runway would not go away. J.D. was conscious of the fact that if he wanted to fly out passengers on intercontinental flights without any restriction on services, he needed a runway some 9,500 feet long. In February, 1978 the then Sir William Elliott (now Lord Elliott), one of Newcastle's MPs pressed Trade Secretary Edmund Dell in the House of Commons for an extension to the Newcastle runway. It was turned down. The Minister said that 'this major extension was not justified at this stage.' So the saga of the Newcastle runway went on and on and was never finally resolved; and today the runway length remains the same as it was at the start of the seventies.

Returning to the Sir Frederick Snow project for developing the airport in the early seventies, a rude shock arrived with the announcement of Government plans to freeze all regional airport development. Government wanted to stop airports overlapping each other and drawing passengers from the same catchment area. The Aviation Authority wanted feasibility studies carried out on dual developments within the same regions; for example, Cardiff and Bristol; Birmingham and East Midlands; Newcastle and Teesside.

In 1973 Alan Stratford and Associates were commissioned to carry out a study by the Civil Aviation Authority with the Airport Committees of Newcastle, Teesside and Carlisle.

One year later,when the Stratford Report was published, the North East Regional Airport Committee and Jim Denyer received a rude awakening. Although the major finding of the report was that Newcastle and Teesside should be allowed to develop independently, preference should be loaded in favour of Teesside so that it could be brought up to par with Newcastle. The report recommended that the only runway extension should take place at Teesside; and that the Civil Aviation Authority should favour Teesside when granting new licences for scheduled and charter services. The resulting increase in traffic at Teesside would be at the expense of the airport at Woolsington. It was hardly surprising that this report struck horror among the members of the authority running Newcastle Airport. The NE Regional Airport Committee strongly objected to the bias in the report, and called for an independent inquiry.

According to Stratford, bias would favour Teesside for a number of years to allow them to catch up with Newcastle, after which both airports would continue with their own independent development. Councillor Bill Collins, then chairman of the Regional Airport Committee, described the Stratford plan as 'an outrageous suggestion'. He argued that on the basis of size of population and catchment area, Newcastle presented a far stronger case for development. The lifelong divide and rivalry between the Tyne and the Tees was rarely better demonstrated than in this battle between the two airport authorities. The Tees airport, boldly advertising itself as 'Teesside International Airport' situated in the centre of North East England, and as the gateway to the region's cities, coast and countryside for the business, domestic or tourist traveller, opened for business at Middleton-St-George in 1964. The Tees boasted about its 'superb 2,291 metre runway', modern handling facilities and its excellent weather record.

It was hardly surprising that Newcastle did not share those aims. J.D. asserted that Teesside, which had converted an old RAF Station into a municipal airport, was restricted in terms of geography and topography by the North Yorkshire Moors on the one hand, and the Pennines in the west on the other. He also pointed out that the catchment area was shared by, and overlapped with airports to the north and south.

The battle for supremacy centred on the strong desire of both authorities to own and run the officially designated Regional International Airport, for in the mid-1970s information started to leak from Whitehall that every municipal airport in the land was to be placed in a category which would determine their future role. As in all major political battles, the outcome may rest on one telling blow, one lightning rapier thrust that is crucial to the outcome. J.D. believed that the blow that brought victory for Newcastle was a meeting between Newcastle's representatives and the Aviation Minister, Stanley Clinton Davies MP. The Woolsington delegation presented their case with such force and vigour that it left the Minister in no doubt about his choice for the regional airport. Newcastle's case included the following four main points:

1. Newcastle was a well established, successful municipal airport whose traffic continued to increase.

2. Newcastle Airport already served the areas stretching from southern Scotland down to North Yorkshire in the south, and across to Cumbria in the west—which placed Woolsington in the centre of the northern region.

3. Newcastle, offering modern facilities, was preferred by most airlines as a regional centre of operation.

4. The majority of northern MPs preferred the Woolsington location to that of Middleton-St-George.

Although the battle had raged for some time, the Government White Paper for the Categorisation of Municipal Airports published in 1978 finally confirmed that Newcastle had won the day.

Awarded a superior category, Newcastle emerged as the Regional International Airport with a mandate to provide medium and short haul scheduled international services; and a range of charter and domestic services including links with the country's gateway (intercontinental) airports. While Newcastle became a Category 'B' Airport, Teesside was graded one class below in 'C' Category, authorised to provide third level services catering primarily for local need and concentrating on general aviation with some domestic feeder services and some charter flights. Since then, Teesside has expanded its international and other flights.

Emerging from the regional war for supremacy as the victor, Newcastle could now look ahead and plan the future with bold confidence. So in 1978 the engineering consortium of Sir Frederick Snow and Partners were asked to evaluate schemes for an expansion at Woolsington which would take Newcastle Airport in the 1990s. By November of that year a visionary development plan emerged that would establish Newcastle in the forefront of municipal airports in England. 'This was a major expansion plan which would enhance the terminal building and the air operations and which was to cost more than £8,000,000. We had to push ahead in order to cope with the ever increasing numbers of passengers,' said the airport manager.

The design called for a terminal extension of over 4,000 square metres and the introduction of the island check-in system, an increase in international arrival facilities, departure lounge space, office and service area accommodation. On the flying side of the airport, the plan called for a change to aircraft 'nose-in parking' with a new pier to provide access at high level and the provision of gateroom lounges. On the operations side, J.D. recalled that he was recommended to expand air traffic control and the briefing building to provide new and separate approach control radar facilities.

The airport managers lost no time in arranging the necessary funding for this large development which was helped by a grant of £2.2m from the E.E.C. Time was of the essence. Passenger traffic continued to rocket and the forecast in 1978 that Newcastle would be handling some 1,500,000 passengers by 1990 turned out to be remarkably accurate. The work pushed ahead and by 9 December 1982 the new £8m. terminal complex was officially opened, providing a flight path for the future, and an example of the vigour and enterprise shown by James H. Denyer and the consortium of the big three county councils who formed the Regional Airport Committee: Tyne and Wear, Northumberland, and Durham.

Years before, to meet the challenge of increasing business traffic, J.D. augmented his airport management by introducing a three-part executive structure. With responsibility to himself as Managing Director were two Assistant Directors, one for operations and the other for finance and administration. In 1973 an appointment was made which was to play one of the key roles in the expanding airport. George Wright of Coventry Airport, ex-RAF and formerly an air executive with the Malawi Government was put in charge of operations at Woolsington; while Eileen O'Kane, one of the airport's most efficient and long-serving employees was put in charge of finance. When Eileen O'Kane required an assistant, an inspired choice was made; Trevor Went, who managed the airport's accounts for Tyne and Wear County Council was brought into the team. This was the same Mr Went who years later was to take over the top job at Woolsington when Jim Denyer retired.

Unfortunately a tragic event took place in 1979 which was to fracture this strong management team—the sudden death of Eileen O'Kane. During a spell of severe wintry weather, she was driving home from the airport after work when she was caught up in a blizzard; during that car journey she suffered a severe heart attack and died the next day. Eileen had been a pillar of strength in airport administration at Woolsington since the 1950s and her death was mourned by all the airport staff, not least Mr Denyer. As a result, Trevor Went was promoted to succeed her as Assistant Director, Finance and Administration. His work impressed the Airport Director. 'Trevor Went learned the ramifications of the airport business quickly. In order to fully appreciate the operational side of the airport, he trained to become a pilot,' said J.D. Later, when the airport became a limited company, both he and George Wright were promoted to full Directors. Another member of the management team, Jim Bainbridge, formerly Mr Went's assistant was appointed Director of Finance when Mr Went was appointed Airport Managing Director in 1989. Grant Riddick was appointed Director of Operations following George Wright's retirement.

At one time the operation of an airport in Newcastle used to cost ratepayers a good deal of money. But by 1982 the airport had been making a trading profit for six years. As the aviation business boomed, Newcastle broke the £1m. profit barrier for the first time. Even hard-headed County Treasurers were taken by surprise by the increase. In 1982, chairman Bill Collins reported that operational income was up by more than £280,000 while income from concessions rose by an extra £135,000—mainly from the duty free shop and the bonded warehouse. The chairman put it this way: 'Newcastle International Airport has already achieved a great deal—the best is still to come!'

The dream that was mocked by the doubters of earlier years had come true...

# Chapter XI

## THE MOMENTOUS DECADE OF THE EIGHTIES

## PIONEERING FOREIGN FLIGHT RETRACED FIFTY YEARS ON—A TIME FOR REFLECTION

The last decade of James H. Denyer as Managing Director of Newcastle Airport was pivotal to the continued success of the now universal air operation taking place at Woolsington.

By the end of 1982 Stage Three of the development, costing more than £8m., had been completed, launching Newcastle into the forefront of municipal and provincial airports in England.

Travellers arriving at Woolsington were greeted by an enlarged terminal building offering very modern systems to speed the flow of passengers. Major improvements were also carried out on the operational side of the complex.

This new-look international airport was now capable of handling 2,000,000 passengers per year; by the time the Managing Director retired in 1989, a new record had been set, numbers soaring to over 1,600,000 per year. In addition, holiday tour operators had now introduced long-haul flights extending to countries like America and Canada.

The new era that dawned for the bustling township of the air called Woolsington was a poignant reminder that the catalyst for this modern aviation development had arrived on the scene exactly thirty years before. When J.D. took up his post as Commandant in 1952, he looked out onto a toy-town airport operation. What a transformation!

The anniversary prompted the Airport Authority to celebrate his thirty years' service with a dinner party, during which he received many congratulatory telegrams including three from members of the Royal Family, the Queen, the Queen Mother and Prince Charles. The esteem in which this airport manager was held was reflected by these Royal messages.

Three years later, in 1985, the airport celebrated its golden jubilee. Fifty years of flying from Newcastle was a proud and piquant landmark for those closely connected with the Woolsington operation. During the celebrations there was a nostalgic look back to the first day of operations, 27 July 1935. When crowds of people started to arrive for the official opening they found themselves in an attractive rural scene where the airport nestled into one small section. The grassy airstrip, hangar, clubhouse, fuel pumps and fire tender garage did not require a very large area in which to carry out operations.

The event prompted a buzz of excitement and an air of expectation among the big crowd who were to be treated to an impressive fly-past by the Royal Air Force and a rare display of trick flying and aerobatics. In addition the public could take to the air themselves via joy-rides offered by the Alan Cobham Flying Circus. Looking back it seems incongruous that some City Councillors were totally opposed to the building of this airport. Opponents argued that in an area suffering from severe deprivation and high unemployment it was scandalous to spend the then huge amount of some £35,000 on an airfield 'which would be little used'.

Although well meaning, these local representatives were men of little vision, unable to look into the future and grasp the significance of air transportation. In the early years making a journey by air was restricted, by cost, to business people, Government officials, and the well-to-do.

By 1939, Pan American Airways had launched the first nonstop regular passenger service from New York to Southampton by Clipper, a luxury flying boat, though it was not yet affordable by the masses. The explosion in air transportation was not to take place until twenty years after the end of World War II.

Back in 1935, Newcastle became the fifteenth municipal aerodrome to be opened in the country—a rather belated arrival if one considers the lead given by Newcastle Aero Club who had already been flying for ten years. Nevertheless, the opening of the Newcastle Aerodrome, initially managed by the Aero Club for the Corporation, was the start of a new era for North East England, bringing air services to the doorstep of the Tyne for the first time. That day in July, 1935 was a never-to-be-forgotten occasion for all who were present. Apart from the Lord Mayor and Corporation, other Civic leaders, the Secretary of State for Air, Sir Philip Cunliffe-Lister, one of the key figures present was Sir Stephen Easten, a Newcastle builder who was the driving force behind the new airfield. It had taken him six years, as chairman of the Municipal Aerodrome Committee to persuade colleagues on the City Council that the new airport would not be a complete and utter waste of ratepayers' money. This visionary Geordie cannot be praised too highly. Unfortunately Sir Stephen did not live to see the commercial and aviation triumph that Newcastle Airport was to achieve; he was dead within a year of the grand opening. A perusal of the minutes of Newcastle City Council for the relevant period is witness to his great determination to succeed with the venture; he would not entertain failure and would hear no criticism of the airport plan.

On the Airport's opening day he stirred the large crowd gathered for the occasion with the message: 'I want to issue a warning—what you have seen today is only a beginning of what we expect to provide here for the Newcastle of the future.' J.D. could not emphasise his role too strongly:

'It is men of vision like Sir Stephen Easten whom we have to thank for providing the nucleus of the modern airport we see at Woolsington today.' The Minister for Air was under no illusion about the difficult part played out by Sir Stephen in forcing through the project in the middle of 'the hungry thirties'. He told the people assembled on the flying field: 'It is particularly creditable that you have carried through on sound lines and with a view to future development, when I know your district has been stricken by the depression.'

A major ally of Sir Stephen had been the Lord Mayor, Councillor R.S. Dalgleish, who had been pursuing an initiative of his own: to try and attract an aircraft manufacturer to build a factory close to the new airport, thus establishing a major aviation centre on Tyneside. To that end he persuaded Anthony Fokker, the brilliant Dutch aircraft designer and manufacturer, to come to Newcastle to discuss the idea. Although Fokker, a world famous figure in aviation, listened carefully to the argument from Newcastle Corporation, nothing came of the idea.

So it was fifty years later that Newcastle, now a thriving international airport, was celebrating its Golden Jubilee. One of the celebrations took the form of recreating the first ever overseas flight made from Newcastle which was to Norway. This flight to Stavanger was something of an epic journey in the thirties when aircraft were still small and aeroengines, though reliable, were of limited horsepower. To blaze a trail from Newcastle to Norway, Allied Airways prepared a de Havilland bi-plane with a carrying capacity of fewer than twenty passengers. Before boarding the aircraft to take off the Lord Mayor of Newcastle christened the aeroplane the *Norseman* with expectation of forging a permanent air link between the two countries. That initiative has stood the test of time. The outward journey was uneventful, but on the return leg the *Norseman*'s radio operator sent telegrams to both Norway and Newcastle to mark the historic event. Stavanger replied in appropriate terms but Newcastle's radio telegram was returned unanswered—Woolsington in those days had no licence to receive 'wires' through the air. But the plane did carry twelve pounds of Norwegian mail destined for northern England.

To commemorate this epoch making flight in 1985, Dan-Air—the airline which had done most to continue the air link with Stavanger—managed to trace the pilot who had flown the inaugural flight in the thirties, veteran pilot Eric Starling of Largs. He and Airport Managing Director Denyer were among the VIPs who boarded the jet plane of the 1980s to relive that unforgettable journey of long ago.

The early days at Woolsington were crammed with memories for J.D., and particularly the first few years of the 1950s. He was soon aware there were many pitfalls awaiting the unwary manager of an airport. One of his early shocks was to discover, while perusing an Ordnance Survey map of

Woolsington, that a right of way path ran right across the new runway system he had laid out to attract the first post-war airline to Newcastle. The reader may be aware that in those days, the airfield was located south of the present site and was adjacent to the present Aero Club Building and hangars. A check with the Newcastle Town Clerk only confirmed that access to the pathway remained and that this right of way had not been removed. Shortly afterwards a telephone call from a retired Army Major living close to the airfield removed any doubts he still had. The airport manager had to live with the problem until the necessary Act was passed revoking the right of way in the early sixties—but the Act applied to the right of way along the course of the runway only. When J.D. retired in 1989 qualified access still remained and the existence of a stile to the north side of the field proved the point! The history of this right of way reveals that it was granted many years ago to afford a pathway from Woolsington village, through the Woolsington Hall area to Dinnington where parishioners could attend Sunday church services.

One story of the fifties which J.D. remembered with mixed feelings concerned a fellow pilot who was unlucky enough to fall foul of the law. The case made aviation history as the aircraft captain, Brian Waugh, became the first commercial pilot to be charged in a civil court following an air crash. The story began in the winter of 1954 when Mr Waugh's company was chartered to fly eight people in his light aeroplane to an event in Dublin. Seven of the passengers were boxers, students from Durham University, who were *en route* to Ireland to participate in a tournament. The aeroplane, a twin-engine DH Rapide had not been airborne long when fate struck a cruel blow: in freezing weather conditions the aircraft crashed onto a fell near Simonburn, Hexham. Incredibly no one was killed. The case that followed in Newcastle Magistrates' Court set a legal precedent, making pilots responsible for 'iced-up' aircraft. Found guilty, he was fined £50.

At the time, and to his dying day, Brian Waugh maintained his innocence, claiming that he had been wrongly blamed for the accident. He alleged that he had been given an inaccurate weather forecast and was not warned of icing hazards. Although Mr Waugh died in 1984 in New Zealand, where he had emigrated with his family after the accident, his son Richard, convinced of his father's case, recently pulled together all his father's manuscripts and was successful in getting a book published. Jim Denyer had fond memories of Brian Waugh whom he rated as a good pilot and companion.

J.D.'s pioneering days at Woolsington formed a treasure chest of memories, and surprises were always just around the corner. The day he agreed to accompany a local pilot on a business trip to RAF Station Silloth began innocently enough. Michael Keegan, a partner in BKS Air Charter persuaded him to make a car journey to pick up a Dakota machine which his company was acquiring. On the day, Keegan, an aircraft engineer as well as a pilot, called for him in his powerful Jaguar two-seater sports car. J.D. recalls: 'When we hit the open road the accelerator went to the floor boards and there it remained. As we flashed along I realised there were only two positions on the throttle, fully open and fully closed. To say that it was a hair-raising drive is not to exaggerate. I leapt from the car as soon as we arrived at Silloth.'

On checking this old Dakota, Keegan and Denyer could not establish when it had last flown, though a Flight-Sergeant assured them the engines had been run up periodically. The machine and the engines seemed in order though there was a question mark about the state of the undercarriage as no retraction tests had been carried out. The two pilots took the aeroplane up and had only been airborne for a few minutes when there was a loud bang from the starboard engine. 'The whole aircraft shook and we quickly closed that engine down. Having reached only 700 feet we decided to raise the undercarriage to gain height, hoping that it would come down again when reselected, which it did. We executed a close circuit and landed safely on the one good engine. We discovered that a cylinder had disintegrated in the Pratt and Whitney engine. The incident could have been worse; when the explosion took place, fragments of cylinder were flying about outside the aircraft.'

After that escapade, it was unsurprising that Denyer and Keegan said goodbye to the Dakota and walked to their car to return home. As J.D. put it: 'I suddenly realised that after facing one emergency in the air, I was to face another little test on the road—a flying return in the Jaguar. After another hair-raising drive, I was glad to get safely back to Woolsington.'

In a lifetime of aviation there are so many stories to tell, so many indelible memories to recall. As an airport manager J.D. quickly learned to expect the unexpected. Each day as he walked through the doors of the terminal building he knew he was primed to deal with any emergency, and the numerous problems that would emerge that day.

Some occasions were more pleasurable than others; he always enjoyed the visits of the Royal Family. In nearly forty years in the 'hot seat' at Woolsington, J.D. supervised the arrival and departure of many Royal flights; the record shows that they all went off without a hitch. The nearest thing to a minor emergency was when Prince Philip, flying down from Scotland in a turbo-prop Andover machine, arrived over the airfield at exactly the same time as the helicopter which had been instructed to pick him up. It goes without saying that the helicopter was ordered to stand by to allow the Andover to enter the approach and land. By the time the Royal plane was down and stopped, the helicopter had landed close by ready to whisk him away to his Tyneside appointment.

Any international airport, by virtue of the many thousands who pass through in the course of a year attracts one or two 'odd balls' and eccentrics. One such person was a little old Tyneside lady, dubbed by the press as the 'Flying Grandmother'. She had a mania for flying but could not afford to buy an airline ticket. Daily she would arrive early by bus at the airport, enter the departure lounge and watch for a chance to nip through boarding onto a plane. She tried it many times, and though she was always stopped, entertainingly engaged the ground staff who took a shine to her. The airline pilots even made bets on who was going to end up with her. Staff noticed that 'Granny' made it her business to collect used boarding passes. One particular day a flight to Jersey had been delayed and ground hostesses could not collate the number of passengers with the number of boarding cards. Captain Ernie Hand, anxious not to miss his flight schedule time into Jersey, decided to depart, requesting the ground staff to sort it out. They soon discovered that the 'Flying Grandmother' had disappeared from the lounge; a radio message asking Captain Hand to check his passengers revealed the little old lady sitting happily strapped to her seat! She shook everyone on arriving in Jersey by asking for a transfer to a North American airline as she so much wanted to visit her daughter in the USA! Although the airlines could not oblige, she was given VIP treatment on the flight back to Newcastle and chauffeured home in a hired car. That was the last anyone knew of the 'Flying Granny'. She was never seen again.

One unusual story from J.D.'s earlier days centres on a commercial pilot called Mahmood; an ex war-time though much prized Dakota aircraft; and a contract to carry the Royal Mail. It all began when the Post Office approached a small charter company, called Air Luton and run by a Captain Mahmood, to fly the Royal Mail nightly from Newcastle to Liverpool. The service had been operating for some time from Newcastle when J.D. grew suspicious about this small company from the South of England, principally because they were in arrears with payment of fees and charges for the use of facilities at Woolsington. Despite being pressed, the company did not settle the arrears. When J.D. checked with the Post Office, they informed him that they had now cancelled the contract with Air Luton as it had got into financial difficulties. On further investigation, Jim found out that the company did not actually own the Dakota was but was lease-purchasing it from another company. That was when the telephone on the manager's desk at Newcastle Airport started to get hot. First Air Atlantique, who had previously operated the service and had leased the aircraft to Mahmood were making claims on the machine. Then an Exeter engineering company rang to claim the Dakota as security for unpaid maintenance work carried out on the aircraft. Another phone call from the south of England was from an unknown pilot who asked to came to

Newcastle to 'test fly the Dakota and check a flap problem'. J.D. had his suspicions about the last call; if he granted the request he could envisage the machine disappearing into the clouds for ever, with a bill still unpaid. The Newcastle Airport Authority, now owed a sizeable sum of money, started proceedings to impound the aircraft, and were successful. There was a sting in the tail for Air Atlantique—to retrieve their own aircraft they were duty bound to pay the Newcastle Authority. That was the end of the affair as far as Newcastle was concerned. No one knows what this lovely old Dakota thought about the machinations going on around her. In the end justice was done. After a lifetime of passenger and cargo carrying, in war and in peace, she ended her days proudly displayed in an American Aviation Museum.

Throughout his management days at Woolsington, one of Jim Denyer's top priorities was good relations with the travelling public. That was why, from time to time, he held 'Open Days' at the airport as well as being associated with RAF flying displays. Air shows in the provinces go back to the years after the First World War when the main highlight displays of aerobatics and trick-flying were performed by highly trained pilots. In Newcastle, these flying displays were established in 1926 by the local Aero Club then operating from the Cramlington Airfield and were advertised as 'Air Pageants'. There was a quest for knowledge and a curiosity among Novocastrians to see these new flying machines in action and they came in their thousands to the Open Days at Cramlington. The Newcastle public has retained its affection for aeroplanes through the years with the result that big crowds have always flocked to Woolsington Open Days.

The provincial air displays led to the inauguration of national air shows produced on a grand scale with Hendon becoming the 'Ascot of the Air' where the RAF crack aerobatic team was always a main feature. After the end of the Second World War, the Royal Air Force inaugurated Battle of Britain Days, staged every September to commemorate the famous aerial victory over the Luftwaffe.

It was for a Battle of Britain Day in the late 1950s that Jim Denyer agreed to organise three aircraft from the Newcastle Club to take part. On the face of it, the RAF request seemed an easy one to meet: his aircraft would fly from RAF Station Acklington and provide joy rides according to the public demand. When he met the RAF organisers and was told that RAF jet fighters would be giving a display of high-speed flying and aerobatics, using the main runway 300 yards away as the display line, he was made aware that he and his pilots were in for an afternoon of precision flying. Jim recalled: 'Two other ex-RAF pilots and myself flew the public in this hair-trigger operation which had to be synchronised with great precision. We flew alongside the Meteor jets in a corner of the airfield where the margins were not great. In today's terms 300 yards from other jet aircraft would become an 'A' Category 'near miss'. As it happened, everything worked to plan and the day was a great success. In fact the public demand to take flights in the three Austers could not be satisfied. 'Queues formed at the start and remained all day. In a clockwork operation, one aircraft loaded up with passengers, while another was taking off and a third aircraft was in its later stages of flight. I have to say that the three pilots, Dave Davico, Neville Coates and myself were totally exhausted at the end of the day, but no more so than the ground crew and engineers who constantly checked the planes and fuelled them from forty gallon drums in a nonstop operation. But it was a thrilling experience for the public.'

A LONG JOURNEY WITH BRITISH AIRWAYS

In one form or another, British Airways has been associated with Newcastle Airport and Jim Denyer for more than thirty years. On 6 April 1959, Captain Jack Jessop flew out of Woolsington piloting the first, twice-weekly, flight to London. As senior captain for the BKS Airline, he was at the controls of a twin engine Elizabethan carrying twenty-two passengers *en route* to the capital. On 6 April 1989, thirty years on, Jack Jessop flew into Newcastle again, though this time in his capacity as a Board Director of British Airways. For after BKS had proved the Newcastle-Heathrow service, they and Cambrian Airways were absorbed into a BEA subsidiary called British Air Services, with the name of North East Airlines operating from Woolsington. Later that name was absorbed into British Airways, the giant carrier of today.

Also on that day in 1989 Jim Denyer was presented with an award from the BA Board to mark their long association, while Captain Jessop presented BA Station Manager, Jim Shields (a long-serving member of the airport staff) with a commemorative shield to mark the historic flight of thirty years ago.

In an association lasting more than thirty years, it would be surprising if differences of opinion between the Airport and British Airways did not take place occasionally. One unresolved matter centred on an argument about introducing a shuttle-service from London to Newcastle. Aware that BA was already operating shuttles to airports like Manchester, Glasgow and Edinburgh, local MPs and businessmen pressed for a similar service to be started in the 1980s. At a board meeting in Newcastle in 1989, BA once more turned down Newcastle's application on the grounds that the total number of passengers carried on this domestic route was too few. In order to begin a shuttle to Newcastle, some 55,000 passengers would have to be handled per year on the London run. BA could not have been unaware of the size of the gravy-train already running between Newcastle and London—a record number of passengers had been carried in the year ended April, 1989, some 340,000, which generated £20,000,000 for BA coffers. However, no one could deny that the BA scheduled service was first-class with modern jets like the Boeing 757s and 767s plus the latest 'fly by wire' A 320 Airbus making some seven rotations daily and offering more than 1,600 seats. To some extent that frequency of service reduced the argument for the commencement of a shuttle service.

Another British Airways idea, which would have boosted the freight arm of Newcastle Airport years ago was the introduction of a 'cargo village', but it never bore fruit. The plan was to introduce nationwide cargo carrying. The aircraft involved was to have been the turbo-prop Vanguard converted to the cargo-carrying Merchantmen. The strategy was for Newcastle to share a load with Glasgow, ie half a load would be put on at Glasgow, the plane would fly south to Newcastle where the second half of the cargo would be loaded, after which the plane would fly into London. This plan was shelved when BA decided to ship major cargo in containers by road at night, to where specialised planes would be waiting at Heathrow to take off for North America and other destinations. For example, cargo trucked from Woolsington at nine o'clock at night would arrive at Heathrow between 3 and 4 a.m. where it was quickly loaded into giant freighters, enabling the freight to arrive in New York in less than twenty-four hours. One local emergency illustrated the speed of the service. J.D. recalled that when a Tyneside ship broke down and made port in the Bahamas, the shipping line said speed was imperative—they were paying the local port authorities some £1,000 per day in berthing and other dues. 'Swan Hunter delivered the spares—a ship's piston and components—to Woolsington one day, and they were being fitted into the ship in the Bahamas the next,' was how J.D. remembered it.

THE PARALLEL TAXI-WAY SKIRMISH

During the late 1970s and the 1980s, J.D. harboured an idea which he knew would improve Newcastle's runway system and save airlines' time—the construction of a parallel taxi-way. At first, the high cost of the project kept it on the back-burner, though the time seemed opportune in 1982, the thirtieth anniversary of his arrival at Newcastle Airport, to introduce it. The airlines would benefit by quicker turnarounds of scheduled services where Newcastle was a designated picking up point. With the approval of the Airport Authority, J.D. put the project before the Civil Aviation Authority; they replied they would favourably consider it if it had the support of all the airlines.

When J.D. met the airline companies to recommend this improvement to the runway system, he was hit by a bolt from the blue—the airline companies would not have it. J.D. recalled that the BA representative led the opposition influencing the decisions of other airlines like Dan-Air, Britannia and Air UK. The British Airways manager argued that the cost of the building of the taxi-way, some £2.1m. , would result in airlines paying higher tariffs to fly into and out of Newcastle. J.D. takes up the story: 'I was more than surprised to hear that. I explained that there was no plan to increase tariffs, and that the Newcastle Authority would recoup the cost by faster turnaround times and increased traffic. My reply failed to convince them and the idea was still born.'

He was determined not to let the matter drop and at each subsequent annual meeting with the airlines, he brought up the subject anew. He re-emphasised the timesaving, indicating that the ground turnaround time for an interconnecting service could be cut to only twenty minutes. They still refused to approve the plan despite the fact that J.D. had already enlisted the support of pilots and operating staff.

The disagreement dragged on until, in 1987, the Manager decided to force the issue. At that year's annual meeting with the operational and financial managers of the airlines J.D. opened up with an admonitory message: 'If you, the airlines, fail to give your support to the project today, it will be shelved by the Airport Authority and the next time it is raised it will be by you, asking us to introduce it. When that day comes, you, the airlines, will pay for it...'

The ultimatum had the desired effect. As J.D. put it: 'There was a deathly hush. The airlines said that they would go away and reconsider the matter. Within three weeks I had received their unanimous support; the CAA gave their immediate approval and at last the new parallel taxi-way system was off the ground!'

It was a fitting climax to Jim's official duties that he should declare the new taxi-way open in 1989—flying in at the controls of a light aeroplane to do it.

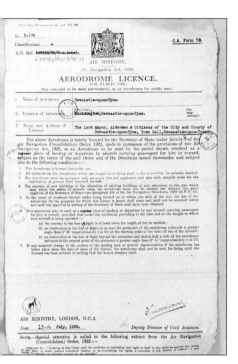

35  The first airport licence, issued 23 July 1936, though the Club opened for business in 1935.

36  At Woolsington in the 1930s. John D. Irving, the Club chairman, second from left.

37  Woolsington crowds watching the RAF flypast of fighter and bomber aircraft at the official opening 26 July 1935.

38  An aerial view of the early airport. The main airport building is now the Aero Club.
Note the aerodrome identification circle on the ground, white painted stone spelling out
NEWCASTLE.

39  Summer 1935, the entrance to the
airport.

40  Newcastle Municipal Aerodrome's
first fire engine.

41 *A winter scene in the post-war years at Woolsington. The wooden control tower on stilts was built and left by the RAF.*

42 *An air display at Woolsington. J.D. Irving and Eileen O'Kane standing at the rear, and Ald. Mould-Graham at the right of Mr Irving. Civic dignitaries and the Lord Mayor, Alderman Norman Chapman, can also be seen.*

43 July 1948. One of the first 'package holidays' to fly from Newcastle. The de Havilland Rapide, belonging to Tyne Taxis Charter, was ready to fly to the Isle of Man.

44 The air-side in the fifties. The Commandant's office is on the corner, while the terminal is the hut between the lighting columns.

45 *Eileen O'Kane. She was a first-class administrator and a great support to Jim Denyer for many years.*

46 *The airport in the early 1950s. In the foreground are Dakotas and two Tiger Moths to the right. At the entrance to the hangar are two DH Rapides. In the background the remains of the RAF camp.*

47 *The first tarmac runway in the mid-fifties.*

48 *A good air-side shot in the sixties. Three Elizabethans can be seen.*

9 By 1971 some of the world's biggest aircraft could be seen at the new airport. This one is a stretched version of the Douglas DC-8.

50 A rare picture of a Spitfire (four bladed propeller) arriving at Newcastle Airport in 1978 as part of the RAF's Battle of Britain Flight.

51 *Part of the Battle of Britain Flight, a Hawker Hurricane.*

52 *The RAF's outstanding bomber aircraft of the last war, the four engine Lancaster.*

53 *The Aero Club's opening day in 1925. Attention is centred on two open-cockpit de Havilland Cirrus Moths.*

54 *The beautiful lines of 'Bernicia', one of the Moths, just prior to take-off.*

55 *Major S.A. Packman, the Club's first flying instructor, pictured with Club engineer Mr J. Brown with a Cirrus Moth outside the Cramlington hangar. Major Packman was killed in a flying accident in June 1926 flying a monoplane, 'The Gull'.*

56 *'The Gull'. Aero Club pilot Baxter Ellis at the controls shortly before Major Packman's fatal flight.*

57  *After the death of Major Packman, 'Parky' Parkinson was appointed flying instructor. He is pictured here with his DH Moth.*

58  *Sir Sefton Branckner an RAF Air Vice-Marshall who became Director of Civil Aviation, at Cramlington with John Boyd.*

W. DUNNING
GROUND ENGINEER

F. P. J. McGEVOR
PILOT INSTRUCTOR

COL. SIR JOSEPH REED
PRESIDENT

F. L. TURNBULL
HON. AERODROME
MANAGER

J. H. BOYD
CHAIRMAN

*Five leaders of the 1930s Aero Club. J.H. Boyd (chairman), F.L. Turnbull (Aerodrome Manager), Col. Sir Joseph Reed (President), W. Dunning (engineer) and F.P.J. McGevor (Pilot Instructor).*

60 *The Newcastle Civil Air Guard, based at Woolsington, turned out some fine pilots in 1938-39.*

61 *After being shot down and captured in World War I Philip F. Heppell was a POW with Baxter Ellis (left).*

62 *The bliss of flying in empty skies over Northumberland. This is the Aero Club's first machine, taken in flight in 1925.*

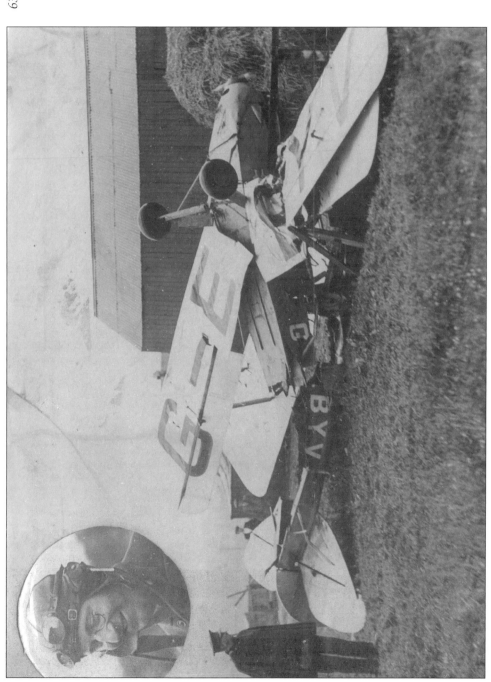

63 The DH Moth which crashed into a farmyard in the 1930s. Pilot Sam Smith (inset) smiles at the thought of his miraculous escape.

64  1928. During a violent storm the roof was blown off the main hangar. Three aircraft were damaged, this one being the worst hit.

# Chapter XII

## A LOVE AFFAIR WITH AEROPLANES

## A TIGER MOTH MAKES KING'S CUP HISTORY

Pilot Jimmy Denyer had many love affairs with aeroplanes in his time, not least with the famous de Havilland 'wonder plane of the war'—the famous Mosquito. But one romance, which was to last longer than all the rest, related to a small light aeroplane which was to become immortal, the Tiger Moth.

The saga of Jimmy and the Tiger Moth is quite rivetting, not just because of the longevity of the love affair but also because of the national record he set in it. In one machine—G-AIVW—he became the only pilot ever to win the coveted King's Cup in a Tiger, an outstanding achievement bearing in mind he was flying an open cockpit 'Biggles' type aeroplane with a very limited top speed.

To put that record into some perspective—for it will never be beaten—it is necessary to look into the history of this remarkable machine. The Tiger Moth started life in the early thirties and it did not take long to establish it firmly as the number one training aircraft. It was produced by aircraft workers at Hatfield, where de Havilland moved their HQ in 1930. Its low purchase price and above all, its supreme reliability, made it an ideal aircraft in which to train pilots to fly. It came from a classic breed of aircraft, its forebears including the DH Cirrus Moth, the first really practical light aeroplane, which had been bought by Newcastle Aero Club when it was formed in 1925.

What made the Tiger Moth supreme in its class was the Gipsy engine which introduced new standards of reliability for aircraft engines. Even so the machine was not one a pilot could take liberties with. Jim's assessment: 'It had the habit of magnifying whatever minor faults a pilot may have. Although it was a gentle aircraft, it was very sensitive...I have seen pilots flying Tiger Moths level out coming into land suddenly balloon upwards: the pilot has gone a little too far back on the stick too early. Instead of the machine being only a few feet off the ground, he suddenly finds himself thirty feet in the air...I have to say though that these handling qualities and the feel of the aeroplane made the machine an excellent training aircraft. Pilots have told me in the past: "If you can fly a Tiger Moth properly you can fly a Spitfire." I agree. The Tiger Moth was a lovely little aeroplane but you could not take liberties with it. If you did, you knew it would kick you up the backside.'

So Tiger Moths became a familiar sight, buzzing around the Newcastle airfield in the late 1930s. With war clouds looming, and tension mounting in Europe as the leader of the Third Reich strutted across frontiers it was not surprising that the Royal Air Force inaugurated the RAFVR (Volunteer Reserve) in 1937.

Here again, the Tiger Moth was given a prominent role in fulfilling the object of this new reserve: training pilots for wartime flying. Young men on Tyneside with an interest in aviation were attracted to the flying club at Newcastle where they received initial training to become pilots. On the outbreak of war, they received extended training before embarking on RAF operations.

Later, but before the outbreak of World War II, the Government introduced a new flying training scheme operated by the Civil Air Guard; this supplemented the role of the RAF Volunteer Reserve. Newcastle Aero Club's Tiger Moths were pressed into service by the CAG, the club receiving a subsidy from the Government. Open to men and women over seventeen (with a liberal cut-off age) the CAG did not lack recruits in Newcastle. The Guard was issued with a simple uniform: denim flying suits with Union Jack flashes sewn on the shoulders.

When war did break out in 1939, the farsightedness of creating volunteer flying organisations reaped its just rewards, with RAFVR and CAG pilots supplementing the comparatively small number of regular aircrew in the Service.

After the end of the war, the use of the Tiger Moth for training pilots did not diminish; flying clubs in this country and abroad employed the machine to train pupil pilots. In the 1950s Newcastle Municipal Flying School was still using the Tigers, and J.D. for one was sorry when Newcastle Corporation withdrew from flying training and sold off the machines.

J.D. spent many flying hours training young men and women to become pilots in Tiger Moths, which he found extremely rewarding. He paints his own picture of what it was like to sit at the controls and fly this de Havilland winner: 'Dressed in leather helmet, goggles, Irvin Jacket and gloves, you climbed into the cockpit of this lovely old lady. After completing pre-flight checks and running up the old Gypsy Major 1 engine, you cleared chocks away and eased into a short take off. With experience, you could estimate roughly what speed you were flying at by listening to the sound of the wind through the wires. I have often come into land without looking down at the air speed indicator, just listening to the wind noise. Coming into land one could hear the beautifully engineered Gypsy engine playing its own familiar tune, the familiar pop-pop, bang-bang noises emanating from the exhaust pipe, which ran below the cockpit indicating that all was well.'

One engaging character who used to fly Tiger Moths out of Woolsington was Ernie Fail, a butcher from Morpeth. He joined the local Civil Air Guard and was a long serving pilot of Newcastle Aero Club, having flown at Cramlington before 1935. In the post-war years, Mr Fail, flying his Tiger Moth G-AHWG, created a piece of aviation history. After the theft of a large number of Christmas trees from plantations at Haydon Bridge and Fourstones, he was asked by the Police to fly a photographer to record the scene of the crime. When proceedings began, those aerial photographs became the first to be used in a criminal court.

Of all the Tiger Moths flown by J.D. the one that stole his heart was the lovely blue and silver G-AIVW, which he first met in 1951. That was the machine he chose to make his debut in national air racing in the 1950s. He used to call it 'Victor Willie'. That was the plane that took him to his first international victory in 1955 (the Norton Griffith's). Looking back, it was a real feat to win 'The Norton' with a standard machine which was one of Newcastle Flying School's training machines. 'Victor Willie' was not in any way 'hotted up'. J.D. had to fly flat out all the way to win—two cockpits, petrol tank located on top centre of the wings and without dynamic fairing. Power was provided by the air-cooled, straight-in-line four cylinder Gypsy Major 1 engine.

When J.D. won his first King's Cup in 1956, he had switched to an Auster Autocrat. Failing to win in 1957 he elected to fly 'Victor Willie' once again in the King's Cup but only after 'souping it up'. He asked his Newcastle engineers, led by Bob Forsyth, to convert 'Victor Willie' into 'a hot-ship'. The Tiger Moth underwent subtle streamlining. The most important task was fairing-in and smooth-lining the rear cockpit. That allowed pilot Denyer to fly from the front cockpit—which altered the centre of gravity and caused a problem on landing. 'I discovered that coming into land with myself in the front cockpit, it was difficult to get the tail-wheel down. The new streamlining was effective so I was determined to persevere,' he recalled. 'I noted that the touchdown was faster and I had difficulty in stopping. As the Tiger Moth had no brakes, the ground crew had to grab the wings after touch down, switching off the engine at the same time!'

The modification had included fitting the Gypsy Major lc. engine with alloy heads to increase compression and produce more power. In the quest to make the machine fly faster, the engineers removed the hard-runner from the wings leaving only the fabric cover which made boarding difficult for the pilot. To assist access, a piece of plywood was held in place over the wing. The petrol-tank was removed from the top centre of the wings and faired in; and the slots fitted to the wings were removed, making landing more difficult. The final touch was to fit a special propeller to synchronise with the high compression engine. The Newcastle crew thus became the first to carry out a wholesale streamline job on a Tiger Moth. Coupled with the skills of pilot Denyer, the team looked forward to the 1958 King's Cup Race with some confidence. The story of that race has been told in a previous chapter, J.D. making his mark by becoming the first pilot to win the King's Cup in a Tiger Moth.

One can get some idea of that achievement by noting that the King's Cup was staged as far back as 1922 when outstanding pilots of the day competed, year on year. Early winners included famous names like Sir Alan Cobham, whose daring survey flights in the 1920s opened up new air routes in Europe and the Commonwealth; and Sir Geoffrey de Havilland, aircraft designer and manufacturer of famous aircraft such as the Tiger, who won in 1933 flying his own Leopard Moth (at an average speed of 139.51 miles per hour).

After the 1958 air races, J.D. continued to fly and instruct trainee pilots in 'Victor Willie' which by that time had returned to normal configuration. Unfortunately, fate was to strike a cruel blow to this favourite machine. During 1960 at Woolsington, a pupil made a serious error coming into land, crash landed and so badly damaged the machine that it was declared uneconomical to repair by the Flying School insurance assessors. It was a sad day for many local pilots when G-AIVW, in pieces, was loaded onto a trailer and dispatched to the headquarters of the Tiger Club in Surrey. From there it was taken to a Croydon aircraft company to be rebuilt into a seaplane on the instruction of one Norman Jones, founder of the Tiger Club.

Before 'Victor Willie' arrived at Croydon for conversion, a former test pilot, Air Commodore Christopher Paul, felt so strongly about the absence of any sea-worthy seaplanes in Britain that he launched an enterprise to form the Seaplane Club, to be centred at Lee-on-Solent. In 1960 if a UK pilot opted for a seaplane endorsement to his pilot's licence, it meant a trip to Norway. Paul was supported by Norman Jones who agreed that Nepean Bishop ('Bish'), the Tiger Club's CFI should be seconded to the newly formed Seaplane Club to help get it off the ground. Thus the British Seaplane Club was born in April, 1963 and the resurrected G-AIVW, after major surgery, reappeared on the Solent as the one and only Sea Tiger.

No one knows what 'Victor Willie' thought about this radical change in its contours and appearance, though one man who followed its fortunes was J.D. As a founder of the Tiger Club and well known to Bish, he was able to keep in touch. When the Seaplane Club folded after some time, the Sea Tiger was welcomed back into the arms of the Tiger Club. For twenty years, it became the only float-plane in the country, though its new career was strewn with misfortune. Twice it crashed into the lake at Calshott though it was successfully rebuilt. The killer blow struck when the Sea Tiger stalled and crashed into the sea off the English coast—the pilot was saved though the machine was never recovered. J.D. stated 'I have to say that this Tiger from Newcastle, of which I became extremely fond, is still lying somewhere at the bottom of the sea. What a sad ending to a lovely aeroplane.' That requiem to old G-AIVW—for no one could change its registered letters—was a heartfelt one from its old pilot.

It would be misleading not to record that during the life of the Tiger Moth there have been numbers of people killed and injured while piloting the machine. It would be surprising if that were not the case. The first machine was built in the 1920s, and the best estimate is that some 9,000 machines of various marques were built, finishing up in various parts of the globe. At the same time, some pilots made miraculous escapes when their Tigers crashed. The best example recalled by J.D. was the astonishing escape of a friend called Lewis Benjamin, who at the time was giving a demonstration of low-level 'crazy' flying during the Sywell Air Display at Northampton in 1963. J.D. recalls that the Tiger flicked into a spin, digging its nose into the ground, bouncing back into the air and then landing very heavily, collapsing its undercarriage and ejecting its engine. One has only to glimpse the photograph taken at the moment of crash to know that this indeed was a miraculous escape. Benjamin was lifted clear of the crash without severe injury, though he did suffer a broken nose, a minor eye injury and bruising. The incredible fact is that he was flying again after a fortnight, though the badly damaged aeroplane was unserviceable for much longer, requiring a major rebuild.

A LOVE AFFAIR WITH AEROPLANES

The man who flew the Tiger Moth faster than any other pilot during the fifties had a number of other favourite machines in an aviation career of some fifty years. Out of fifty types of aircraft registered in his log book, J.D. had a soft spot for the aeroplane that won him his first King's Cup in 1956. That was a high wing monoplane , the Auster Autocrat, G-AJRH, fitted with the reliable Gypsy Major engine and bearing the lucky number 7 on the tail plane. It was not all that fast at straight and level, the Gypsy engine producing only 120 brake horse power, about the same as an upmarket saloon car of today! J.D. recalls that once airborne, it sounded like a flying sewing machine. But in the skilful hands of the experienced pilot called Denyer, it was able to beat the best pilots and machines in the country in the King's Cup.

His love affair with aeroplanes began in earnest at the age of seventeen when he was accepted into the wartime Royal Air Force to train as a pilot. He learned the rudiments of flying on the Miles Magister, and one sharply-etched memory was flying this little twin-seater on his first solo flight. 'That I will never forget, coming in to land I could see other cadets watching to see if I was going to fluff my landing—without an instructor. Thank goodness I got it right,' recalled J.D.

One aircraft that had a special place in his recollections is that immortal machine, built by the Douglas Aircraft Corporation of America, the Dakota, as we came to know it, though in America it was the DC-3. When the prototype of this celebrated machine was being drawn up in 1932, Jim was only nine years old. In the following years, Douglas developed the DC-2 in 1934 but the quantum leap was made in 1935 by the introduction of the DC-3.

It was an immediate success, and its long life extends up to the present day. During the 1980s, two Dakotas were flying out of Newcastle, one operating the Royal Mail Service. As late as 1990, an Air Atlantique Dakota was using Newcastle Airport during North Sea Coast anti-pollution patrols. The flying workhorse was primed to spray chemical dispersants on any oil slicks that might appear.

The Dakota is arguably the most successful aeroplane ever built. It was the first machine in its land of origin that made it possible for airlines to operate at a profit without the need to carry mail. In so doing, it revolutionised air transport, this attractive twin-engine aircraft setting a new standard for passenger travel. The machine had a flexibility of use. Through the years it has carried countless numbers of passengers on feeder routes throughout the world; it has been used as a freight-carrier; during war-time it has been used to tow fully-laden gliders, and to carry paratroopers during attacks—this was the plane that did the big drop at Arnhem. It was also widely used during the Berlin airlift. J.D. accumulated many flying hours in the Dakota over the years. He flew it at Ringway, Manchester when the machine was used for training paratroopers. He flew it into Berlin in 1948/49 to help defeat the Russian blockade. He realised during that airlift just how good a puller the Dakota was; it was put into service to carry large loads of freight for which it was never intended. 'I have to say that the DC-3 was and is a delightful aeroplane. Although by today's standards it is quite slow, it will do all you ask of it and has an outstanding safety record.'

If you asked J.D. to nominate one or two favourite machines from World War II, he put the de Havilland Mosquito in the top bracket. This was the aircraft that surprised the aircraft design world of the day—instead of metal, it was made of wood. Consequently, it could be manufactured in large numbers, employing armies of workmen skilled in joinery and woodwork. 'I flew with No. 29 Squadron in Mosquitos in low level operations over Germany and found it fast and manoeuvrable, the twin Rolls Royce Merlins thrusting it forward at speeds up to 400 m.p.h. Its weaponry also packed a punch,' said J.D. He did have a small reservation; the two-man crew did not have much room. In the two-seater, the seats were fitted almost side by side and it had only one door, next to the navigator. In an emergency, the pilot could not disembark until the navigator had exited. 'It was still a lovely plane to fly'. The Mosquito, one of the most versatile of World War II aircraft, was used in various roles including that of fighter, pathfinder, and light bomber.

Another night-fighting machine which J.D. had time for was the Bristol Beaufighter. This all-metal, twin-engine monoplane may have had a limited top speed without the manoeuvrability of the Mosquito, but it was as hard as nails and extremely reliable. 'I've seen Beaufighters return to base after a mission riddled with bullet holes and still flyable,' recalls J.D. It carried a greater armoury than any other fighter, including multiple cannon. As in all night-fighters employed on air interception and using AI Radar, the closest co-operation was demanded of pilot and navigator. In the Beaufighter, the seating was not ideal; the pilot sat in front, and his navigator—with his radar screen in front of him—sat behind the bulkhead and the pilot could not see him. He could only hear him against aircraft noise.

Another aircraft that he remembers well was the Avro Anson, a single wing twin-engine machine which was used for pilot training. J.D. remembers: 'I flew Ansons at RAF Ouston during the war and they had one or two characteristics which I won't forget. One related to the manual, retractable undercarriage. I recall that it took 130 winds to get it up, requiring a very fit second pilot!'

Two outstanding machines from World War II were the Spitfire fighter and the Lancaster bomber. He was able to fly them both after the war, describing both flights as 'unforgettable experiences'. Of the Spitfire he said: 'What a wizard plane that was, a dream to fly. As soon as you touched the controls, the machine was off, obeying every command like a thoroughbred—and what power from the Rolls Royce engine.' He flew the powerful, four-engine heavy bomber Lancaster as pilot in command—a very different experience from flying night-fighters. 'It was rather eerie being in command of such a large aircraft, but despite its size, it handled like a lady in the sky. The same machine could bomb the hell out of the Germans.'

# Chapter XIII

## A SALUTE TO WOMEN PILOTS

## EARLY HEROINES OF THE SKY

Long before the dawn of equal opportunity, a small band of women in the 1930s set countless hearts beating with their daring exploits in aviation. A select few became internationally famous, flying enormous distances round various parts of the globe; often they flew alone, crossing hundreds of miles of ocean in rather primitive aeroplanes with little or no back-up on the ground.

In various parts of the country during those early days, small groups of young women could be seen donning leather jackets, helmets and goggles, climbing into de Havilland Moths to learn the business of flying. Although they may not have become internationally known, these daring young things helped to thrust forward the new frontiers of aviation. Here at the Newcastle Aero Club of the 1920s were a tiny band of women who were proving at the Cramlington Airfield that women could fly just like men. Jim, after a long career in aviation, which included a period of instructing pupils in Newcastle has no hesitation in saying that a good woman pilot can hold her own with any male pilot.

He talked in admiring terms about one particular woman pilot, who flew at both Cramlington and Woolsington. Constance (Connie) Leathart was in fact a pioneer of women's flying in Newcastle upon Tyne. She was the first woman to fly from Cramlington in 1925, the year that the Aero Club was founded. Jim went on to say: 'Connie, who's still living at Little Bavington in Northumberland, is a lovely lady, and I can recall her flying her own plane with great expertise when I arrived at Woolsington in 1951. Only the passing of time caused her to pack up flying and sell her dear little aircraft some years later. She flew for more than thirty years, was a keen competitor in air racing, and during World War II joined the Air Transport Auxiliary, ferrying war planes around for the Allied Services. Connie was in at the beginning all right, and flew alongside such famous names as Amy Johnson whom she knew quite well.'

There were several other women flying from Cramlington before 1930, though their number remained small. The prerequisites for flying then were to be rich, or at least comfortably off, owning the necessary transport to get to the airfield as there were no buses or other services in the beginning. Because of the sparsity of women fliers in the early days women from different flying clubs got to know one another quite well, visiting each others' airfields whenever racing or air displays were held. One such woman aviator was Winifred Brown who, although hailing from Manchester, became a familiar figure at Cramlington before 1935. J.D. recalled that this woman pilot attained a signal honour in air racing—she was the first and only woman to win the King's Cup. She pulled off this coup for women in July, 1930, piloting an Avro Arain aeroplane, G-EBVZ, powered by a Cirrus marque 3 engine and flying the course at an average speed of 102.7 m.p.h. To mark this triumph, Newcastle Aero Club decided to present Ms Brown with one of the most handsome and valuable racing prizes in the country—the Newcastle upon Tyne Trophy, made of gold and silver. Specially made for the Newcastle Club, this magnificent trophy included a flying motif resplendent on a golden globe, supported by the outstretched arms of beautiful ladies gazing towards the sky. The trophy, presented by Sir Joseph Reed, President of the Aero Club, was bought with monies donated by Northcliffe's *Evening World* (one of two Newcastle evening newspapers of the time). Lord Northcliffe, an outstanding benefactor of aviation development, directed that some £1,500 be donated to the Newcastle Club 'for the purpose of encouraging civil aviation'. It proves the value of the trophy that it took much of that to have it made.

On the international scene in the 1930s, a handful of women pilots were making aviation history by their daring exploits, setting up new records in long-distance flying over different continents. J.D. had no hesitation is saluting the deeds of women like Amy Johnson, Jean Batten and Amelia Earhart. That pioneering trio became known as 'The Daughters of the Sky', achieving an almost Hollywood style charisma with the public. For them, danger was a lure rather than a deterrent. 'These women pilots were pioneers in their own right,' stated J.D., 'breaking records and catching the imagination of the public by their feats in low-powered aeroplanes with primitive navigational aids. Some of the earliest record-breakers flew in open cockpits, following a visual course with maps strapped to their knees. Flying thousands of miles alone, without any mechanic to handle an emergency is awe-inspiring.'

Amy Johnson, a typist from Yorkshire, was the number one among women pilots, according to J.D. 'Amy must occupy the premier position among women pilots for her feats of long-distance flying over sixty years ago. Her achievements were an inspiration to many other women, starting them to think about taking up aviation for themselves.' Amy Johnson got into flying by learning about aircraft engineering at the old de Havilland Stag Lane Aerodrome in north west London before taking lessons to fly. After winning her pilot's licence, she decided to prepare for a record flight to the other end of the world—Australia! By the summer of 1930 she was ready, and took off from Croydon in a DH Gypsy Moth bi-plane, engaging the elements from an open cockpit. During the course of that nineteen-day flight, she flew blind through sandstorms, over featureless deserts, across hostile territory, with gale force winds sometimes buffeting her little aircraft all over the sky. At one point she was forced to land with engine trouble, but successfully carried out minor repairs before arriving safely in Brisbane—to became the first woman ever to fly to Australia. Later she went on to break more records.

J.D. clearly recalled hearing the tragic news of Amy going missing one day in 1941. During the war, she had joined the Air Transport Auxiliary and her flying duties included delivering planes to the RAF. On the fateful day, she was ferrying a military aircraft over the Thames Estuary in bad weather conditions when she went missing. She was never seen again and was presumed drowned. Amy was 'the Queen of the Air' between the wars, songs were written about her and the public took her to its heart. She was only thirty-seven when she lost her life. By her outstanding achievements in flight, she had proved that women pilots could be as capable and determined as men.

Another woman pilot who rated highly with J.D. was Amelia Earhart, who startled the world by demonstrating that a woman could fly solo across the Atlantic. That was a very daring feat in 1932 when transatlantic planes were in their infancy. The many hours in the air needed to cross the Atlantic could be a dangerous business then. Earhart, an American, went on to set numerous flying records in her own country. Her last fatal flight in 1937 entered the realms of mystery. In an attempt to fly round the world with a companion, her plane was lost over the Pacific and she was never heard of again. That is until more than twenty years later when a report from America claimed a section of her aircraft had been found on a remote island in the Pacific. The theory was that she had made a forced landing and died of thirst. 'No one can be certain what motive prompted these women to put their lives at risk, time and again, to fly mammoth distances across oceans and deserts, but one has to admire their bravery,' concluded J.D.

It would be a serious omission not to mention another British woman aviator who became an international celebrity in the early thirties. Peggy Salaman was a fine example of 'the bright young thing' from the wealthier classes who brushed all danger aside to set a new record for light aircraft flying between London and Capetown. She did that in her little single engine de Havilland Puss Moth. Then there was that other outstanding woman flier, Jean Batten, whose exploits in her de Havilland Gypsy Moth thrilled the public in the thirties. Her epic flights were from England to Australia, both ways, though she made other headlines with her adventurous flights over British Empire air routes. She also created a new speed record for flying from England to South America. Although this young woman was a New Zealander, she came to London to learn to fly and to generate sponsorship for her record-breaking attempts. A woman with film star looks, she always flew alone and overcame great mishaps to set up new records, surviving two crashes on her Australian flights. She made those arduous journeys without radio, navigating by compass and a long roll of concertinaed aerial maps. J.D. put their achievements into perspective: 'What you have got to remember is that these women were launching their daring exploits when long-distance flying was in its infancy. They climbed into open cockpits and defied the worst of the elements and all manner of danger to set the nation's pulse quickening.'

In more recent years, another woman pilot hit the headlines, though by the 1960s great strides had been made in the manufacture of light aircraft, as well as equipment. Nevertheless, the record-breaking solo flight around the world in her small Piper Comanche in 1966 was a major achievement for Sheila Scott, who became the first British pilot—man or woman—to fly round the globe solo. She twice crossed the equator covering a distance of more than 30,000 miles in thirty-three days. Later, she set other records including London to South Africa in 1967. J.D. got to know Sheila Scott well during his air racing days, describing her as an excellent pilot who lived for flying and soon became a well-known racing pilot. 'Her achievements were enormous, though you have to remember that in the sixties she flew with many advantages over pioneers like Johnson and Earhart,' he said. 'Good women pilots can hold their own with men pilots and the trend is for more women fliers to be taken on by the RAF and some commercial airlines. Whether women will make fighter pilots in times of war remains to be seen.'

RHODA OF 'THE FLYING HEPPELLS'

One woman who proved the capability of women pilots to fly alongside men in the Royal Air Force is Rhoda Fairbairn of Gosforth, Newcastle upon Tyne. She made history more than forty years ago as the first woman pilot to fly with the RAFVR. After Mrs Fairbairn was accepted by the Service as air crew, she rose in rank from Sgt.-Pilot to Pilot Officer and finished up flying Hurricanes and Spitfires. Her inspiration to fly aeroplanes stemmed from her father, the late Philip Forsyth Heppell, one of the pioneering members of Newcastle Aero Club who never lost his zest for flying. As a Royal Flying Corps pilot in World War I, he was forced down over enemy lines and taken a prisoner of war. Rhoda's brother, Whaley Heppell was a much-decorated fighter pilot during World War II, while Rhoda herself flew with the Air Transport Auxiliary during that war. J.D. speaks highly of 'The Flying Heppells', father, son and daughter, all wartime pilots.

The aviation career of Rhoda Fairbairn began as war clouds gathered towards the end of 1939. The Government introduced the Civil Air Guard, a force to train civilian pilots who could be called on if war broke out. Rhoda applied to join the CAG, was accepted and began to learn to fly in an old DH Moth at Woolsington. The vast majority of pupil pilots were men; the only woman flier, apart from Rhoda, was a young woman called Trixie Lister. There was no male chauvinism, the two lone women were totally accepted; in fact the male instructors were vying with each other to get their own pupil to pass out first. You could say that Rhoda was born to fly aeroplanes; she went solo after eight hours of instruction and showed all the skills required to make a good pilot.

While flying from Woolsington, Rhoda was involved in one minor crash. Coming into land one day she was buffeted by a sudden wind change, causing one wing tip to hit the runway, flipping the plane over. Apart from a smashed propeller, no other serious damage was done to plane or pilot, though Rhoda does not forget that day easily, as her diary entry for November 29 1938 shows: 'First crash today, turned the machine upside down coming in. I escaped injury, Mrs Lester gave me a coffee and I had a ride back to the hangar on the fire-engine!'

Rhoda Heppell was under twenty when she learned to fly, and it was a happy day when she was awarded her pilot's licence by the Civil Air Guard. However, when she decided that she wanted to join the war effort, she found that the gargantuan military machine of HM Services could move in mysterious ways. When she applied to join the ATA to ferry aircraft, she was not accepted. Apparently she did not have enough flying hours in, so instead of flying planes she was driving military vehicles in the First Aid Nursing Yeomanry. Later, while stationed at York, she heard that the Air Transport Auxiliary were now accepting people with fewer flying hours. 'Imagine my delight when I applied to join the ATA and was accepted,' she recalls. As a result of that, Rhoda found herself in something of a pickle: she was still in the FANY who knew nothing of her bid to transfer to the ATA. By good fortune the man at the Air Ministry who had to sort out the problem was none other than J.D. Irving who had been Aero Club chairman before the war, and soon Rhoda was sent to Waltham Aerodrome near Maidenhead.

After further pilot-training and conversion courses she flew Miles Magisters and Hawker Harts, carrying out reconnaissance on West Coast aerodromes in readiness for ferrying aircraft to them. A typical day's work with the ATA would see pilots pile into an Anson at White Waltham, which would drop them off at various airfields and factories in readiness to pick up aircraft for delivery. Ferrying war machines was very worthwhile job though it entailed much hanging about at strange airfields, waiting to be picked up after making a delivery. One of the attractions of the job was the chance to fly a wide variety of machines. Apart from Magisters and Harts, Rhoda flew at least fifteen different makes of aircraft including the

Spitfire, the Hurricane, the Hawker Hind, the Fairchild, the Anson and the Harvard.

There were one or two major war-time problems facing ATA pilots like Rhoda Heppell. They had to beware of the balloon barrages protecting cities from enemy air attack, and they were also vulnerable to the vagaries of the British climate as they carried no radio to receive intelligence. The Air Transport Auxiliary made a valuable contribution to Britain's war in the air; records show that more than 300,000 ferry trips were made during the war years.

The war had been finished for some five years when Rhoda was seized with the desire to get back to flying. Reading an advertisement in a local newspaper one day asking for flying recruits for the Royal Air Force, she applied and was accepted. In 1950 she was posted to RAF Ouston for retraining, returning to a whole new world of flying machines where radios, navigational aids and superb instrumentation were standard fittings. A far cry from the old DH Moth with its open cockpit she had flown at Woolsington before the war. Now at Ouston she was rubbing shoulders with a new breed of fighter pilot, and new challenges in flying modern machines were presented. One experience she will not forget. After training on low-level flying, the order came through from sector HQ to commence new training at zero feet! As Rhoda said to herself: 'I could hardly believe it, now they have gone really barmy. But it actually happened.' Commencing zero-feet flying, the instructor would yell: 'Keep her down, keep her down, up over the hedge, keep her down!…We flew so low, I felt that the thorns from the hedge tops were going up my backside. Then I got the taste for this dare-devil flying. Of course, it was highly dangerous, flying at ground level among hills and lakes. It was impossible to see other aircraft around you and you could easily collide…We flew at nought feet for quite a while and then the message arrived from HQ at Rufforth, York, that a mistake had been made. We should have been flying at one hundred feet, not nought feet!…I have to say that to my amazement, there were no crashes at nought feet and no one got hurt.'

Later, when a new major conflict threatened Britain, Rhoda applied for a commission and became a Pilot Officer. She remained with the RAFVR for some years, ending up flying Meteor jet machines and concluding her days as a Service pilot only when age demanded retirement. In the 1990s, when a handful of women are vying to become the first fighter-pilots of the regular Air Force, it is worth remembering that Rhoda Fairbairn from Gosforth was setting the pace for women volunteers in the Royal Air Force more than forty years ago.

# Chapter XIV

## AVIATION—THE POWER GAME

## THE INSIDE STORY OF THE RISE OF
## NEWCASTLE AIRPORT

If power-play is necessary to achieve success in the razor-keen competitiveness of the world of aviation, Jim Denyer as an airport manager realised that political adroitness and dexterity were imperative for the job. In nearly forty years as the chief executive of the airport, he fenced, thrust and parried with politicians at all levels, from local councillors to Members of Parliament and Government Ministers. He discovered that he possessed an ingenuity which allowed him to win over leaders in Whitehall and Westminster.

When he started his management of Woolsington in 1952, he did not have an easy time to begin with. He was keen to push ahead with airport expansion including runway development—and soon discovered that red tape could put a spanner in the works. His masters then were Newcastle Corporation. The fact was that Newcastle Airport was then a loss-maker and City Councillors were wary of injecting ratepayers' money when there were so many other urgent calls on city finance, particularly in a run down post-war situation.

Fortunately, Jim was helped by a far-sighted chairman of the City Airport Committee, Col. Robert Mould-Graham. Between them, they provided the dynamic which slowly began to transform Woolsington from a rural, sleepy little airfield into the modern airport of the sixties, although the major development had to wait until 1963 when local authorities got together and formed the North East Regional Airport Committee. Only then could the huge finance necessary to build a new, modern terminal be found.

He soon discovered that with the formation of this new regional authority the power game of politics was to be played anew. With the coming together of first five local authorities, later joined by another two, the whole representing areas on both side of the river and in two counties, it was inevitable that there would be a play for power. J.D. saw it all happen from the inside with County Durham winning the day, and installing their own inaugural chairman, Andy Cunningham. Teesside was nowhere to be seen. They had already decided to go their own way and run their own separate airport.

Hats off to Newcastle, Gateshead, South Shields and the counties of

Durham and Northumberland for leading the way in the new consortium. They were soon to be followed by Sunderland and Tynemouth. However, the man at the sharp end of the airport operation, manager James Denyer had now to sit down in committee with more than twenty local councillors. Encompassed by a small army of local politicians, many a manager would have bitten the bullet and gone with the consensus for an easy working life. Not Jim Denyer. From the beginning, he made it plain that as the only aviation professional he expected to make decisions and get the support of the committee. If he succeeded, and he felt certain he would, the bouquets would fall into the laps of the councillors. If he failed, he would take the brickbats. With a supportive chairman he began to set the agenda which would eventually lift Newcastle into the top ten airports in the country.

Some planners were dismayed that Teesside had decided to go it alone and open up their own airport at Middleton-St-George, causing a split in the overall regional development and diluting finances which might have been available to create one master airport for the North East. On the other hand one can understand the view of an independently-minded Teesside who thought that Woolsington was too far North; the Teessiders wanted an airport close to their own industrial and business heartland. By 1964 when services began at Middleton-St-George, the clarion call for a single major airport for North East England, located at White Mare Pool, had long since faded out. Looking back, it is astonishing to discover that plans for a 'dream airport' at White Mare Pool were first laid in 1929. The idea lay dormant for years until the plan to develop the site was revived by Transport Minister Frank Pakenham in 1949.

The site had much to commend it; it lay between Newcastle and Sunderland with road and rail access, with the option of opening up new roadways into the south of the region. Featuring three runways and a plan for an impressive terminal building, it could have become one of the finest airports in the country. There were some drawbacks. Critics pointed to the presence of mining subsidence and industrial haze. In the event, neither Newcastle nor any other major local authority emerged as champions of White Mare Pool, and a Conservative Minister for Aviation later killed the plan off.

In the ensuing years, Jim Denyer played a key role in the battle to establish the premier airport for the region—was it to be Newcastle or Teesside? That story has already been told, though it has to be said that J.D.'s political 'nous' and Whitehall contacts played a significant part in the emergence of Woolsington as the winner. The Government categorisation of regional airports in 1978 sealed the fate of Teesside, making Newcastle the region's number one airport, and grading it above its southern neighbours.

As Newcastle fought to overcome the huge capital costs of

modernisation, the year 1976 was the financial turning point for the airport; for the first time income exceeded expenditure and also covered capital repayments. By 1980, a healthy financial surplus was recorded even though the costly Stage Three development at Woolsington had begun. The North East local authorities, who had injected risk capital in earlier years, were about to reap their reward.

J.D. recalled that while attending an overseas' aviation conference, the then chairman of the Airport Authority, Bill Collins, told him that he had in mind a 'dividend' payment to authority members, at the same time retaining funds for capital development. In fact the 'dividend' issued was £1m. and every year since has exceeded that sum. According to J.D.: 'By 1988, monies distributed in the form of dividends exceeded all local authority airport expenditure since the formation of the North East Regional Airport Committee.' That was at a time when other major capital commitments had been taken on: £2.9m. towards the cost of the Metro rail link, and £2.1m. for the new parallel taxi-way. The repayment of dividends proved to be a good political move, and was an election vote winner for the constituent local authorities as J.D. saw it.

The next major political move, which had serious consequences for the North East, was the abolition of the Metropolitan County Councils. When Tyne and Wear C.C. was abolished in April, 1986, the airport local authorities decided to share out the nest egg that had been built up between them. 'The annoying thing was that when Tyne and Wear CC was finally run down, the surplus was almost identical to that they had transferred from the airport funds,' J.D. said. 'I told them that was airport money which we had worked very hard for. However, the fact was that the airport was local authority-owned and you couldn't argue with it. Since the airport became a private limited company, money has been put aside annually for the replacement of assets.' (The first meeting of Newcastle International Airport as a private limited company took place on 27 March 1987).

So the flight of aviation politics continued almost straight and level until the emergence of turbulence caused by new government thinking about who should run municipal airports. It now promised to be a case of fastening seatbelts for a bumpy ride. The Government plan concerned the question of introducing private capital into local authority airports. That would give private companies seats on the airport boards with the possibility of a major share holding falling into private hands. During this political power-play, J.D. was questioned by Whitehall 'mandarins' about the operation of the municipal system. He told them bluntly that after many years at the sharp end, he could report the system worked well.

Later on he suggested one or two qualifications. 'While it could be said that some councillors who have served on committee have no real business experience, and may be influenced by their own independent councils, the councillors themselves are first-class people who learned quickly about aviation matters. Perhaps it wouldn't hurt to have some outside influence on the board; one advantage would be that funds for development would be easier to obtain from the money market.'

So the situation today is that Newcastle Airport is run by a private limited company—which is not quite what it sounds. The Airport Board is made up solely of representative councillors of local authorities, as it has been for years (plus of course the full-time managing officers). There is little private about it—North East authorities own all the shares and retain 100 per cent control. Private investors cannot buy into the concern. Government attempts to involve the private sector were cleverly defeated by the consortium of regional local authorities.

That political coup d'état is intriguing. To understand its significance, it is necessary to understand Government thinking of the time. The Department of Transport *Airport Policy Report 1985* (later to become the Act of 1986) favoured the redefining of airport categories, with the accent on flexibility rather than rigidity. Aviation services should occur naturally as a result of the operation of free market forces. The document argued that the running of regional airports by joint local authorities was not the most efficient way of operating the business. As a lever to force airport committees to sell shares to private companies, the Government made it difficult for local authority boards to obtain capital finance. Nevertheless, local authorities took a stand and seizing on a loop-hole in the 1986 Act were able to foil the Government objective of involving the private sector. When the Airport Act of 1986 received the Royal Assent it stated that companies to be formed by local authorities should be linked to shareholding and registered under the Companies Act. It did not specifically compel local authorities to go public and form PLCs. The result was that the Regional Airport Authority took the opportunity to form a private limited company in which North East authorities owned all the shares. So the Government plan to inject private capital into the country's municipal airports failed to materialise. J.D. put it this way: 'The object of the Act was subverted by the local authorities, and in Newcastle's case seven authorities comprising the previous Regional Airport Committee retained full control.' One can understand the reluctance of North East councillors to lose control of their own airport—especially after treading a long hard route to success.

# Chapter XV

## LOOKING BACK ON FIFTY YEARS OF FLYING

## A TREASURE HOUSE OF MEMORIES

To remain at the top in the pressure-cooker world of aviation management for nearly forty years calls for a special breed of man. James Henry Denyer, in his time, has been called caring, determined, engaging and precise.

In the power-play job of international airport management, where decisions can affect lives, he did not suffer fools gladly. He could ruffle feathers among the pompous and high-minded if there was good cause. Confronted by red tape and officialdom, he was known to unleash verbal thunderbolts to get a job done, though a highly persuasive manner was often enough for the bureaucrats. The opinion of all who worked under him was that he was a fair-minded, born leader, who looked after his staff. He had come from the bottom and worked himself up to the top; the one-time apprentice sheet-metal worker who won a commission in the Royal Air Force before becoming an Airport Chief Executive.

His achievement in aviation was reflected by the tributes paid to him by British airport managers and others at a glittering farewell dinner held in the banqueting hall of Newcastle's Civic Centre in 1989. Airport managers representing no fewer than twenty airport authorities subscribed to a presentation silver salver. It was no ordinary salver: engraved were the signatures of every airport director, the configuration of his favourite light aeroplane, Tiger Moth G-AIVW; and the inscription, 'To J. Henry Denyer, OBE, Airport Director Extraordinaire.'

Long before this farewell occasion, James Henry Denyer had become a name in British Civil Aviation; he was known as the 'Father of British Airports', his seniority recognised by BAA, the Airport Operators' Association and British Airways. It explained the large gathering for his farewell, a nostalgic occasion for many, including old Royal Air Force air crew, pilots and professionals from airport management whom he had got to know over the years. The diners included civic leaders, MPs, and leaders of business and industry. As J.D. put it during his farewell speech: 'In the words of the old Cockney song: "We've been together now for thirty-seven years and it don't seem a day too much".' It hardly seemed possible that this pocket-dynamo called Denyer was entering final approaches for a last touch down. The 'landing' was faultless, as usual, only to be expected from a pilot with a log book recording more than 5,000 flying hours.

He told the gathered throng that day that Woolsington had come a long way since the 1950s, especially in passenger transportation. In 1952 the airport handled some 5,000 passengers compared with 1,500,000 in 1989. It was true that in 1952 the airport comprised a grassy runway and some old war-time huts and a hangar. 'Though to put this into perspective, airports nationally were rather primitive. Heathrow was a conglomeration of huts on the north side while Gatwick was still in the beehive,' he told diners. He reminisced that during his career in airport management he had met the President of the United States, most of the Royal Family, every Prime Minister from the fifties to the eighties as well as personalities and leaders from the worlds of entertainment and industry, from Marlene Dietrich to Mohamed Ali, from Lord Thomson to President Carter. J.D. recalled that in the sixties a young man knocked on his office door, representing the consultants engaged to develop the new terminal. 'His name was Norman Payne who's come a long way since then. He's chairman of BAA today. On another occasion, a businessman called to see me to discuss car hire facilities at the airport. You know him as Colin Marshall, now chairman of British Airways.'

Then there was the story of how Dan-Air got started. Davis and Newman, the London Shipbroking Group had acquired a Dakota aircraft and were uncertain what to do with it. J.D. recalled 'When I was asked my opinion, I replied "Why don't you operate it!" They did and that was how Dan-Air became one of our biggest carriers, going from strength to strength in Newcastle.'

They say that behind every successful man, stands a good woman. Jim told the large audience at the farewell that he owed much to his wife, Mary. He went on: 'Mary has helped to organise my life. I've lost count of the many scribbling pads she's gone through to give me reminders for the following day.' He had to admit he had greatly changed her life. 'I met Mary Graham at a RAF Woolsington dance in war-time; a slip of a girl of sixteen, she was a seamstress employed by Fenwick's. Since our marriage two years later, Mary has had no choice but to live a life of aviation, both military and civil.' Although Mary soon became accustomed to being a pilot's wife, one baptism of fire she will never forget. 'I was absolutely terrified the first time I went up in a plane,' she said, 'though I soon became air-minded—I had to be as our family life revolved around flying!' Having acquired the taste for aircraft and aviation, Mary took many 'flips' with her husband at the local flying school. And when he began his air racing career, she caught the buzz and excitement and became one of many hands who helped to prepare her husband's racing aircraft.

She must have felt a touch of sadness when the time for Jim's parting and farewell from Newcastle Airport arrived, though neither she nor her husband were aware of the extraordinary plans being drawn up in secret to make his last day at the airfield a memorable one. It was an old RAF aircrew colleague called Alan Taylor who dreamt up the idea to send him off in royal style by organising a fly-past of modern war planes. Whether this set a precedent to honour a civilian in this way, no one is quite sure. Mr Taylor, of Whitley Bay, who had flown in the same squadron as Jim during the war, No. 29 Mosquito Squadron, had been a friend for years, so he took it for granted that he had every right to approach the Commanding Officer of No. 29 Squadron in 1989 and to ask him to 'put on a show' for an old squadron member. Alan was successful, and along with aircraft offered by other squadrons, organised a fly past of seven: four Tornados, a Phantom, and two helicopters from RAF Boulmer.

On the night of the airfield farewell party, Jim, Alan and friends were taking refreshments outside the marquee, when promptly at 7 p.m. the roar of jet engines could be heard approaching Woolsington. Alan Taylor recalls: 'Jim looked into the sky and said "What's this?"' He knew soon enough: the aircraft put on a magnificent fly-past over the airfield. Two Tornados circled for a second pass, injecting re-heat and soaring to 10,000 feet in what seemed like a couple of seconds. As Alan remembers: 'That made his day. It shook him rigid and he was bowled over. It was a tremendous moment for him.' The final flourish was the appearance of a Cessna light aircraft over the airport towing a 'Farewell Mr Newcastle Airport' sky sign. He would never forget that gesture from pilots of his old squadron.

Looking back over his years as a pilot he would also not forget the role of ground crews, in both military and civil flying, the boys who kept the planes in the air. In the case of civil aviation where millions of passengers fly each year in the UK alone, how many give a thought to the unseen crews on the ground? They may not be the glamour boys of aviation, but their role is vital. The speed and efficiency of aircraft turnaround at any airport can also be defined in terms of time and money. The quicker an aircraft is refuelled, revictualled and loaded with passengers and luggage, the more time and money is saved.

In the world of aviation, Newcastle has for many years been well-known for aircraft-handling. As far back as 1982 the magazine, *Airline World* recorded an interview with the crew of Concorde on its first flight into Woolsington. Their verdict: 'The best service we've ever experienced.' That expertise was in demand when NATO held a mammoth military exercise over Germany, and Newcastle Airport was used as an embarkation stage for British troops. Bearing in mind that the airport was operating normal flight schedules, the additional load demanded handling a three-day shuttle service to Northern Germany, turning round nine Boeing 747's which ferried 4,000 troops and their equipment within three days. The turnaround—including embarking 400 soldiers a time plus equipment, refuelling and servicing was an astonishing forty-seven minutes!

Jim's flying experience in the Royal Air Force in war and peace affords a valued judgment on the work of the ground crews of the RAF, for example the role of the RAF tradesmen at war. Only those who took part in the battle against the Luftwaffe and other hostile air forces will retain vivid memories of the pressures to keep our planes in the air.

In this country, fighter squadrons were often put out to dispersal away from the main aerodrome, to render them more safe in the event of enemy attack. These dispersals and satellites were manned by the ground crews who in winter lived rough and incommodious lives, often on windswept sites with only discomfort to look forward to when their duty was done. In the vice-like grip of a severe winter the sleeping shelter was a draughty Nissen hut, heated by a single cast-iron coke fire in the centre of the billet. It was a testing business at the start of a day to come out of the Nissen into a snowstorm to collect water from a single standpipe protruding from the ground.

All the trades needed to keep aircraft flying may have lived spartan lives, but duty was always efficiently done. When squadrons were stood down a minimum of planes had to be kept at maximum readiness. The view of former night-fighter pilot, Denyer: 'No matter how good a pilot you are, if you have not got a good back-up ground crew you have problems. The engineers, mechanics, fitters and electricians, to name but a few, are of paramount importance. The pilot also relies on the reliability of the ground crew to help his confidence when he is flying a machine to its limits over hostile territory.' An example of close harmony aviation is the *modus operandi* of the well-known 'Red Arrows' aerobatic team of the RAF. Jim states: 'They are as one. Exceptional pilots are backed up by excellent engineering staff.'

If they are the élite of the RAF, the 'erks' who are the run of the mill Air Force tradesmen should not be the forgotten ones, for British ground crews are as good as any in the world. The opinion of J.D. was that the American Army Air Force also set high standards among its squadron ground crews, though there was less formality of rank between pilots and ground crew. 'In the RAF during my war-time years, although discipline was exercised between the air and ground, there was also an affinity between the air and ground crews.'

The illustrious history of the Royal Air Force owes much to the Marshall of the RAF, 'Boom' Trenchard, known as 'The Father of the RAF' who some eighty year ago recognised the need to create corps of excellence on the ground if his aeroplanes were to perform well in the air. His masterstroke was to institute a corps of technical learning at RAF Halton where the Apprentices' School won worldwide recognition. At Halton, fourteen and fifteen year old boys with a aptitude for skilled trades were turned into the fitters, riggers, engineers, mechanics, and electricians who serviced the RAF planes so efficiently through the years. Sir Hugh Trenchard became the first Chief of the Air Staff in 1918. 'Halton produced very competent, highly-skilled aircraft tradesmen whom pilots could rely on implicitly' stated J.D. In peace and war first-class ground crews are an integral part of any air force's striking power.

Whenever J.D. is asked if he thinks that RAF pilots are supreme, he replies that they are certainly among the best in the world. 'The reason I say one air force is not supreme is because it infers that other air forces, like that of the United States, are inferior and they are not. But I have to say that the RAF Central Flying School is one of the best, if not the best, training ground for flying instructors.'

As CFI at the Newcastle Flying School, J.D. also took time out to teach one or two outstanding pupils how to air race. One of then was Stan Jours who won a major award, the Kemsley Trophy, the first time he entered. Later that same year, flying his Percival Proctor in another air race he was lucky to escape injury when a plane crashed immediately in front of him. J.D. who was at the races and saw the accident says he will never forget it. In a tightly-packed take-off, the aircraft alongside Jours failed to get properly airborne, slipping on to its back. The Newcastle pilot, intent on watching the starter's flag, did not see the crashed plane on the other side of him—incredibly his wing overlapped and narrowly missed hitting the wreckage.

There are countless stories that J.D. could have told from his treasure house of aviation memories. Forty years have gone by since the day he was appointed Newcastle Airport Commandant, though anecdotes came flooding out in the resonant voice of a pilot used to clear speaking into aircraft R/T sets. The man did not seem to have changed all that much; beneath bushy eyebrows, the quick pilot's eyes remained. As he looked back on his long career in aviation, he took pleasure from the scene of his accomplishments: the leading role Newcastle has played among the country's municipal airports; Newcastle's launching of the nation's first provincial Air Training Centre for air hostesses and ground staff; the bringing of major tour operators to Woolsington to fly direct fully-inclusive holidays abroad; and the reputation that Newcastle won in aircraft-handling among the provincial airports. They are to name but a few.

Looking back on his private life over the airport years, J.D. kept coming back to the role of his wife, Mary, a constant support in his arduous job. Apart from involvement in aspects of his extensive aviation life, Mary Denyer found time to raise two lively lads, Vivian and Michael. J.D. always placed great value on family life, and took great delight from the company of his five grand-children. No-one can say that the Denyers do not have aviation in their blood. At the time of writing both Vivian and Michael

1   *Aerial view of the airport, showing the new taxi-way opened by Jim Denyer in the year of his retirement.*

2   *Some of Newcastle Aero Club's machines. The beautifully proportioned French-built four-seater, single-engine aircraft named Tampico (foreground) can be seen. Flight office and clubhouse are to the rear of the apron.*

3 Vivian Denyer at work in Air Traffic Control.

4 Concorde after landing at Woolsington in the mid-1980s.

5   Sharing a joke with Prince Charles.
6   The Royal logo painted on the fuselage of an aircraft of the Queen's flight.
7   Jim Denyer talks to the Queen Mother.

8  *Princess Diana bids farewell to Jim Denyer after a visit to Newcastle.*

9   *Jim Denyer enjoys a joke with the Princess Royal in the company of the Lord Lieutenant, Sir Ralph Carr-Ellison.*

10  *President Jimmy Carter on an official visit in the 1970s.*

11  *The Prime Minister, Harold Wilson, after opening the new complex in 1967. Pictured here: Dr Harry Russell, vice-chairman of NERAC; Andy Cunningham, chairman; the Prime Minister; Jim Denyer.*

12 Vivian and Michael Denyer with Jim. Following in their father's footsteps, both sons work at the airport.

13 *Aviation colleagues of peace and war-time at a farewell dinner. Left to right: Alan Taylor ex-No. 29 Squadron; Bob Forsyth ex-chief engineer of Newcastle Aero Club; Geoff Knox ex-Squadron Leader; Frank Burke ex-Manager Dan-Air; Jack Jessop ex-BKS pilot; Jim Shields British Airways Newcastle Manager.*

14 *One of the highlights of the presentations was a front page facsimile of a special edition of the* Evening Chronicle *which bid 'A fond farewell'. Presented by the Editor Graeme Stanton.*

15 The last public appearance of Jim Denyer seen here with his wife at the opening of the Denyer Lounge at Newcastle International Airport. Standing left to right: Cllr. Joe Hattam, (chairman); Alexia Wheeler; Trevor Went, (Managing Director); Grant Riddick; Mike Finch; Jim Bainbridge.

work at Newcastle International Airport, while granddaughter Nicola Denyer (age seventeen) is a Sergeant in the Air Training Corps, intent on winning a flying scholarship to RAF Cranwell with a view to making aviation her career. Memories of family holidays at the Denyer 'hide-away' on the Northumberland Coast were treasured. 'Beadnell has been a favourite little resort for my family; we had a caravan there for over twenty years before buying a second home' he said. Leisure over the years for J.D. included boating, fishing, swimming, skin-diving and scuba-diving. During his airport years he found little time for reading, apart from trade journals and aviation regulation updates. On television, his favourites were news and current affairs (regional and national), cowboy films and weather forecasts from any channel. Obsession with the weather stemmed from his working days when up-to-the minute, accurate weather reports were vital ingredients for the job. In his retirement, he compared local and national forecasts with those prepared by the Woolsington 'Met. Men'.

For years, the Newcastle Aero Club attracted him one or two nights a week, either 'taking a jar' with cronies and fellow pilots, or putting the cue to work on the green baize of the pool table. Latterly he only flew occasionally, with friends. 'After years of being paid to fly, it goes against the grain to have to pay to go up!' he said with a smile. It would be misleading to suggest that J.D. led a life of complete leisure after the day of his retirement; his need for an appointments diary did not go away.

He preferred to remain in the North East region, even though his roots lay in London and Kent, and over the years he formed a close attachment to the people and places that make up this part of England. His eyes lit up when he eulogised some of the personalities and characters he had got to know. Of all the counties, he acclaimed the county of Northumberland in particular. His picturesque little bungalow at Darras Hall was strategically situated to observe aircraft movements in and out of Newcastle Airport. 'I have no inclination to leave this part of the world. I love it. I have made many friends and after all these years, I consider myself an adopted Geordie' (he was once presented with a 'Geordie Passport'). That was how he summed up his romance with the region.

Surveying Jim Denyer's career in aviation, it is not surprising that over half a century he witnessed a revolution taking place in the field of commercial aviation. He pointed to the introduction of the jet engine as the big breakthrough, enabling larger and faster aircraft to be built. Journeys that once took days, took only hours with the fast jets. There was a social revolution in holiday-making too—the big jets opened up holidays abroad for all for the first time. In his fifty years in aviation, this remarkable aviator lived through it all, from the Avro Ansons and Airspeed Oxfords, each carrying six people, to the giant carriers like the Boeing 747 Jumbo, carrying more than 400 passengers.

# Chapter XVI

## A HISTORY OF NEWCASTLE AERO CLUB
## - PIONEERS OF CIVIL FLYING

## THE ROLE OF JIM DENYER OVER FORTY YEARS

Newcastle upon Tyne Aero Club, instituted in 1925, is one of Great Britain's pioneering light aeroplane clubs. When it was launched at Cramlington, Northumberland, private flying was in its infancy. In those barn-storming days, flying meant open cockpits, leather jackets and helmets, goggles and gauntlets, in empty skies with the sound of the wind whistling through the struts and wires. It is a matter of pride for J.D. that he had been associated with the club, in one way or another, for over forty years, and was the longest serving President. When he talked about the early days of the Aero Club, he spelled out the vision of the tiny band of men who came together to launch it; men like John Boyd, a Newcastle solicitor; W. Baxter Ellis, a local corn merchant, and Philip Heppell, a city estate agent. The thread that drew these men together was that they were all ex-servicemen who yearned to fly again. They had all seen service in World War I either with the Royal Flying Corps or the Royal Naval Air Service.

When they first met to discuss the idea of a flying club in 1924, they were a little ahead of their time—no suitable and reliable light aeroplane was on the market to enable a private Aero Club to get off the ground. As it happened they did not have to wait long. By 1924 the Air Ministry was aware of the enthusiasm for flying building up in the nation which coincided with a Government drive to develop a public 'air-sense'. The Air Ministry was only too well aware that Britain would need ready-trained pilots if and when another war broke out. To facilitate such plans, the Air Ministry was looking for design of a hardy light machine with a maximum of reliability, and at a cost which would bring it within the range of those who owned a small motorcar. The breakthrough came in 1925 when the de Havilland Aircraft Company introduced the first of the famous Moth DH 60 bi-planes—and fitted them with the reliable Cirrus engine. It was an immediate success.

Thus was the light Aero Club movement born, and Newcastle was in at the beginning—one of the first five clubs in the country to be registered by the Air Ministry. The others were located in London, Lancashire, Yorkshire and the Midlands. Although Boyd, Ellis and Heppell were at the heart of things they were quickly joined by another eight local enthusiasts; these were people such as Arthur George, a well-known Newcastle motor-trader; Alex Bell, a commercial traveller who became Secretary; L. de Loriol, a city merchant and John Bell, a local schoolmaster. The founder members numbered eleven in all and represented a cross-section of Newcastle life. These members included Brian Dodds, a local printer; Alexander Peacock a wood-turner; N.S. Todd a draper; and W.H. Leet a jeweller. Led by chairman Baxter Ellis, this body of would-be fliers were soon to discover that difficulties and disappointments were to be the order of the day rather than the exception. They called themselves 'The Council of the Newcastle Aero Club', and if they were not well financed they had a steely determination to see the project through.

It was true that the government of the day agreed to give all light aeroplane clubs a subsidy—but so great was the financial challenge in the fledgling years, they were almost overwhelmed by the huge costs of setting up an aerodrome from scratch, from building hangars to buying new flying machines. Although they were able to take over the old RFC airfield at Cramlington, it was rather derelict and needed vast sums of money spent on it. The first priority was to build a new hangar but estimates showed it would cost a fortune, which the sum of £400 was in those days. Finding the finance to equip the airfield was a constant source of worry to the members of the Council. 'A serious menace to one's piece of mind' was how John Boyd put it at the time. A hangar they had to have, finance they had not got. Electing not to shirk the challenge, though with no guarantee of any money, the club informed the construction company: 'Build that hangar—you'll get our money all right.' In the end the money was found from somewhere, as much to the surprise of the builders as it was to the club.

Having acquired an aerodrome and a hangar, the Newcastle club was in a strong position to ask the Air Ministry for money. It is not surprising that in view of their enterprise and with the backing of leading lights in the aviation world like Sir Sefton Branckner (appointed Director of Civil Aviation) Newcastle was successful.

A contract with the Air Ministry was signed as follows:

1. An award of £2,000 for the purchase of two aeroplanes.
2. £500 per annum for two years towards expenses.
3. £10 per annum for each member who qualified for an 'A' licence on club aircraft.

The Ministry inserted a clause which protected their investment for a period of two years: all that the Newcastle Aero Club possessed, or received, was vested in the Air Ministry by way of a mortgage.

The way was now clear for Newcastle to take delivery of their first flying machine, a prospect which generated much excitement among club members. The big day was set for 15 September 1925. On that red-letter day, the thrilling sight of a brand new de Havilland Moth—resplendent in Club livery of red and silver—approaching the Cramlington runway on 'finals' for the first touch-down was never to be forgotten. The bi-plane, Cirrus Moth G-EBLX was piloted by Baxter Ellis, the chairman of the Newcastle Club. Two weeks later, another brand new flying machine, a sister of the first, G-EBLY arrived at the Cramlington airfield putting the Aero Club firmly into the private flying business.

Archives in the Tyne and Wear collection show that aviation interest in the North East region had manifested itself much earlier, though the first Aero Club was short lived. The Northumberland and Durham Aero Club, headquartered at Boldon Flats (which in 1910 was extensive grassland lying north of Moor Lane between Cleadon and East Boldon) was largely concerned with the study of the new science of flying, and its implications for the region. Most of its members were industrialists, scientists and engineers, and in fact after only three years the Club merged with the Institute of Engineers and Shipbuilders. However, there was some flying from Boldon Flats and several air displays were staged. Unfortunately, the first air display organised by the Club ended in tragedy. On August Bank Holiday 1910 the star attraction was a crack woman pilot from France called Madame Franck. She lost control of her Farman bi-plane machine and crashed onto the Boldon grassland, fatally injuring a young telegraph messenger, Thomas Wood and injuring some of the crowd. The pilot escaped with a broken leg and other injuries and was taken to Sunderland Infirmary. In 1913, the Aero Club lost its identity.

To return to the Newcastle Aero Club, the next imperative was to fix the day for the official opening at Cramlington. The chosen date, 21 November 1925 was to be the start of an era of light aeroplane flying which would place Newcastle upon Tyne firmly on the aviation map of the United Kingdom. The official opening of the club was performed by the Lord Mayor of Newcastle, Councillor Anthony Oates supported by members of the Corporation and a distinguished gathering of Newcastle leaders. From that time onwards there was great activity on the airfield with flying tuition being given daily.

'The next anxiety was what to do with members and visitors when they were not flying' reported John Boyd at the time. Cramlington then had neither a mess nor a Clubhouse. The blackened ruins of a one-time officers' mess was but an eyesore. The club leaders decided that the best plan was to rebuild the mess once used by pilots of the Royal Flying Corps, though the cost would be high, and beyond the resources of Newcastle Aero Club at that time.

Two philanthropic members of the club came to the rescue, Messrs P.F. Heppell and R.N. Thompson who said they would bear the cost of the project. The Club could repay them when it was in a position to do so. 'Soon the club-house was a place of comfort, mirth and merriment, and a steward and stewardess were employed' states the Club official record.

Things were buzzing at Cramlington now and there was an eagerness to make Newcastle one of the top flying clubs in the country. Major S.A. Packman, Chief Flying Instructor, took the aspirations of the club to heart and spent all hours passing on his skills and enthusiasm to pupil pilots. It was a tragedy that Packman was to become the first pilot to be killed at Cramlington. On the morning of the fateful day an unusual looking machine called 'The Gull', a small experimental 6 h.p. monoplane, had been flown by Baxter Ellis and Philip Heppell prior to being taken to Druridge Bay to race against motorcycles. Heppell and Ellis had reservations about this underpowered machine which had a tendency to hunt as the pilot tried to fly straight and level. When a Press photographer asked the two pilots to take it up again and fly low for pictures, they refused. Mr Packman told the photographer he would oblige. He flew it round the circuit and was almost back on the aerodrome when it stalled at a height of about twenty feet and crashed into the ground, killing the pilot. Major Packman's body was laid to rest with military honours in Cramlington Churchyard on Sunday 27 June 1926, witnessed by a large concourse of mourners.

Two months later a new Chief Flying Instructor was appointed, J.D. Parkinson who played a prominent part in Newcastle Aero Club's first 'Annual Flying Meeting' held at Cramlington on Saturday 4 September 1926. That was a red-letter day for the club, which was one of the first light aeroplane clubs to stage air racing events. It attracted prominent aviators from different parts of the country, including two former winners of the King's Cup—Air Force fliers H.S. Broad and F.T. Courtney who carried the rank of Captain in those early days before the RAF changed to its present ranking system.

A large crowd gathered at Cramlington to witness no fewer than ten flying events as well as an exhibition of stunt flying by the King's Cup pilots. Highlights of the meeting included the President's Cup Race for 'pilot instructor of approved aeroplane clubs' (Challenge Cup presented by Col. Sir Joseph Reed); and the Open Handicap which attracted aviators from London, the South East, Yorkshire and the North East.

The twenty-mile course was designed to test pilots' skills flying in every direction with ever changing winds. From the start line, the fliers took off due north to High Ewart Cottage, turned sharply south east to Stannington Church, turning again to fly across the aerodrome south east to Cramlington Church, back over the cottage and returned to the finishing line. Prominent Newcastle Aero Club members who were involved in the Race Day included J.W. Leech and Thomas Todd (Stewards), Arthur George and John Boyd (Judges), W. Baxter Ellis (Handicapper), J. Bell

(Clerk of the Course), Brian Dodds (Starter) and Alex Bell (Club Secretary). Local pilots had a successful afternoon. Representing Newcastle in the Inter-Club event were J.D. Parkinson, T.R. MacMillan and N.S. Todd, while Dr H.L.B. Dixon featured prominently in the Inter-Club scratch event.

This inaugural air race day (and others like it elsewhere) could not have taken place without the design and marketing of the little 'wonder' aeroplane that revolutionised private flying—the immortal de Havilland Moth powered by the 27/60 Cirrus Engine. Their numbers dominated the meeting with J.D. Parkinson—at the controls of the G-EBLX—turned out in its red and silver livery, winning the President's Cup for Newcastle.

There was plenty of crowd interest for two machines which were newcomers to Cramlington: the de Havilland 51A, 120 h.p. Airdisco entered by Air Commodore J.G. Weir; and the Martinsyde 300 h.p. Nimbus entered by Colonel Ormonde Darby.

Some of the races carried a first prize of £20, a not inconsiderable amount for those days. J.D. Parkinson worked for Berkshire Aviation Tours as a joyriding pilot before coming to Newcastle. With that company he logged more than 4,000 hours and carried 40,000 passengers without mishap. He had an engaging personality, and formed a wide circle of friends at Cramlington. By 1927 light aeroplane clubs in Britain were strong enough to form their own associations and here again Newcastle was one of the early members. A pillar of the Newcastle Club and its President, Sir Joseph Reed, of Horton Grange near Blagdon, was elected first vice-chairman of the Association of Light Aeroplane Clubs. Newcastle now had a voice in the development of civil flying with the Association meeting regularly at the Royal Aero Club.

Accidents and plane crashes can never be entirely eliminated from any airfield operation, and Cramlington was no exception. In the same year that Major Packman was killed, the club's DH Moth G-EBLY crashed and was written off, though fortunately no one was killed. That was replaced by a third Cirrus Moth bought second hand. Records show that this machine was in service for only two years before it met its end while being flown by a club member in a landing test. After that, the first AVRO aircraft made its appearance at Cramlington, a bi-plane fitted with a Renault engine producing a speed of eighty m.p.h.

The catastrophe that shook the club in 1928 was not man-made but almost totally destructive for all that. In the winter of that year during a violent storm, gale-force winds blew in the hangar roof which fell on top of the club's three machines chocked up for the night. The shock was worsened by the realisation that club funds were insufficient to carry out necessary repairs. The fighting spirit and indomitable will to surmount any challenge once again manifested itself among members. They raised the cash themselves and all three machines were made air worthy again.

During these early years, it was a source of pride at Newcastle that their flying tuition fees, at £1 per hour, were the lowest of any. That rate was held until 1930 when a reduction in Government subsidy caused the club to raise the rate to 30s. per hour. That sum was outside the scope of many would-be fliers, so fewer lessons were taken, and one or two members dropped out. However, the hard core of members remained. The élan and airmanship of Newcastle trained pilots had shown them to be among the best in the country. By 1930, according to the club manual, Newcastle held the record for the number of aviation prizes won by flying clubs in England. Indeed in 1929 club members performed a hat trick of wins in national air racing in one afternoon. The trophies won were: the Grosvenor Cup (Pilot, G.S. Kemp); the Air League Cup ( Norman Todd); and the , Society of British Aeroplane Clubs' Challenge Cup (Dr Dixon).

The expansion of the flying club movement was rapid. In 1925 the associated clubs trained twelve pilots to achieve licences out of 800 members of all classes with 700 hours flying time. By the end of 1930, more than 1,200 members held 'A' licences out of a total of 5,808 members, with a flying time totalling over 29,000 hours. The movement awakened the public interest in flying and air transportation with thousands of people all over the country owing their baptism in flying to the clubs.

In Newcastle in 1931 the annual subscription for pilot members was £3 3s.; for observer members, £2 2s. ; and for associate members, £1 1s. In addition, there was a joining fee of the same amounts. Official charges laid down by Newcastle Aero Club in 1931 were:

> Dual or solo flying £1 10s. per hour
> Joyrides from 7s. 6d.
> Landing fees 2s. 6d.
> Hire of hangars for private owners £10 per annum

By this time the club offered tuition on three DH Moth aeroplanes fitted with Gypsy and Cirrus engines. The club offered pupil pilots a half hourly rate of 15s. solo or with instructor, which was the cheapest in the country. The prowess of the Newcastle Aero Club was such that the Director of Civil Aviation for Great Britain (Mr F.C. Shelmardine) was prompted to write: 'It is gratifying to know that the Newcastle upon Tyne Club—which occupies an honourable place among pioneer clubs—is going from strength to strength.'

One young woman at Cramlington made local aviation history by becoming the first woman to fly on Tyneside. She joined the Newcastle Aero Club in the year of its inception, 1925 and went on to win her pilot's licence by 1927. Her training was interrupted by the tragic flying accident which killed her instructor, Major Packman. She was somewhat stunned by that fatal accident. 'That rather put you off flying, you think your instructor is some sort of God,' she said. Nevertheless, she completed her training under the supervision of another instructor who arrived to help out. Records show that Connie Leathart was among the first twenty women pilots in the country.

That was quite a feat, remembering that she made her mark in the male-dominated world of the 1920s. The stirring exploits of the great women aviators, Johnson, Batten and Earhart did not take place until the following decade. There is an intriguing little story about how Connie Leathart joined Newcastle Aero Club. After hearing about the inauguration of the club in 1925, she obtained an application form, completed it and signed it 'C.R. Leathart.' After some time she was informed that she had been accepted as a member of the club, and was told to forward her first subscription. She filled in her cheque, again signed it 'C.R. Leathart' and posted it. It was not until her first visit to the airfield that she realised there was something odd about her reception—the club hierarchy thought they had admitted a man! However, she was in and became an enthusiastic member of the club.

Having broken the ice for women members, two other aviation-minded local women followed Connie's example: Nora Trevelyan of Nether Witton who joined in 1928, who bought and flew a D. H. Moth; and Sheila R. Matthewson of Hebburn who also became a pilot and remained a member for some years.

In those far off days, the highlights of clubs' calendars were the staging of open days and 'Air Pageants' in which pilots from other parts of the country would take part. Air racing was a magnet which often drew large crowds to Cramlington Airfield. As a result of inter-visits by clubs, Connie got to know some of the outstanding women pilots of the day. One of them was Winifred Brown, a crack pilot from Manchester, who became a familiar figure at Cramlington, having good friends living in Newcastle. Later Connie got to know and became friendly with Amy Johnson, the 'Queen of the Skies'. Miss Leathart recalled: 'Amy was a ground engineer at the Stag Lane headquarters of de Havilland and was learning to fly at the same time. As soon as she got her licence she made ready and took off for Australia. Goodness knows how she got there but she did. She had plenty of guts and was a very nice person.' That was a considered opinion of Amy Johnson, made to the author by Miss Leathart sixty years after Amy set the world alight with her record flights. 'Amy sometimes flew into Newcastle and there is a picture of her arriving at Cramlington after she lost her way!'

Another contemporary woman pilot, though American, was the record-breaking Amelia Earhart. On one occasion when Connie flew into the airfield at Fraserburg to join a party of Cramlington pilots on a joyriding spree, she was stopped by a local as she climbed from the cockpit. 'Miss Earhart, this is a shorter trip than you have been used to, isn't it?' For a second Connie was nonplussed, then realised she had been mistaken for Earhart. Connie did meet Jim Mollison, the well known aviator who married Amy Johnson. 'He was very amusing and had a most beautiful voice' she recalls. Connie was asked to compare men and women pilots in her day. 'I don't think there was any difference between the two. I remember Dr Dixon asking me if I liked men better than women pilots. Well, the idea to make a comparison never occurred to me; it was all fairly simple in those days, not like today,' she reflected.

Flying in the 1920s may have been by the seat of the pants but it was a joyous, almost romantic affair in which owners fell in love with their machines. It was made more exciting by the absence of navigational aids and instruments—pilots flying cross-country took out their maps and followed rivers and railway lines *en route* to their destination. That worked pretty well, though on occasion the system failed, such as the time members of Newcastle Aero Club were invited to attend the official opening of the Blackpool Flying Club in 1928. On the day, three aircraft flew out of Cramlington led by the club's professional instructor, J.D. Parkinson (with more than 4,000 flying hours and a product of the Central Flying School). The flight to Blackpool was without incident, a good time was had by all; Dr Dixon won the Inter-Club Members' Race and Connie Leathart won a prize at the meeting, though the men were soaked with water after taking a ride on the water chute. Without a change of clothes, the men spent the rest of the time in their pyjamas. It was all good, clean fun!

It was on the return journey that the Newcastle party ran into trouble. Whether they had wined and dined too well, no one can say. The fact was that the lead machine with 'Parky' at the controls was slowly getting lost. It all went wrong when Parky led the three aircraft along the wrong railway line. Realising his error, he signalled to the other pilots he was going to make an unscheduled landing on the next large field. After landing safely, Parky left his plane to make enquiries about where he was. He put the question to a farm worker whom he came across. The local told him 'Little Orton, Sir' Parky asked, 'Where's Little Orton?' The local replied 'Near Great Orton, Sir.' Becoming exasperated, Parky said 'Where's Great Orton?' At last came the answer he wanted: 'Four miles from Carlisle Sir.' Somewhat relieved, the Newcastle pilots jumped into their machines, took up their new bearings and were soon touching down at Cramlington. On that occasion, Connie was flying her Grasshopper machine, though in more than thirty years of flying she owned a number of different aeroplanes. They included machines like the Spartan, the Widgin and the Swift. When the Newcastle Club moved to Woolsington in 1935, she continued to fly with them until 1958 when she called it a day, finally selling her aircraft. Today her name can be found on the Honours Board in the Woolsington club house for early successes in the air.

Looking back on the 1920s she admits it was mostly the better-off women who could afford to fly. 'We didn't think too much about flying then, we just did it, though really it all depended on how rich you were. If a woman couldn't afford to fly she could appeal to someone like Lord Wakefield to help out.'

There may have been only three women members in Newcastle then, but by 1931 the number had risen to seventeen. Apart from Connie, their names as listed in the 1931 official handbook: Nora Trevelyan, Sheila Matthewson, Maud Allan, Elsa Grey, Mrs D. Heslop, Mrs F. Irving, Miss M. Johnston, Lady M.L. Leith, Mrs A.E. Ellis, Mrs Mary Middleton, Miss M. Stevenson, Mrs Mina Todd, Miss G. Davidson, Mamie McBryde, Lady K. Parsons and Mrs Tomkin.

Connie recalls that her flying training was completed by Lord Ossulston, ex Royal Naval Flying Service who came to Cramlington to help out after Parkinson, the instructor, departed for a new post in Canada in 1928. The youngest pilot at Cramlington was Lawrence Middleton, who learned to fly at the age of fourteen but had to wait until he was seventeen in order to get a licence. Dr Peter Burnett, of Ponteland, the doctor to Newcastle International Airport for many years, knows Connie Leathart well. He recalls that she once told him that she was good friend of Amy Johnson, and had in fact stayed with her the night before her ill-fated flight for the Air Transport Auxiliary during the war.

Another anecdote Connie recounted to him concerned a close call she experienced when she had to land on a Greek island just after the close of World War II. At that period, the Greek Islanders were suffering the deprivations of war, especially a shortage of food. As an ATA pilot she was given the mission of flying in food to the near-starving islanders. Although Connie carried out the mission perfectly, after landing on a strange island runway she was met by a hostile crowd of islanders. What happened next showed Connie Leathart at her best: with great strength of character and fearless bearing she scolded the islanders for their threats—and pointed out how silly they would be to jeopardise much-needed food supplies. The opposition wilted, Connie completed her delivery and flew out of the island none the worse for wear!

She remembers the huge crowds which used to attend the air displays at Cramlington in the 1920s. Her copy of the *Aeroplane* magazine of 13 June 1927 gives a detailed and colourful account of an Air Pageant at the local airfield. Reported by Charles Grey, the account talks of a crowd of 10,000 with 500 cars and more than £700 taken in gate money. Apart from races and competitions ('Baxter Ellis flew a DH 53 painted a bilious yellow with silver wings and named *Belco*') there were displays of aerobatics and trick-flying. Grey reported: 'Parkinson, the instructor, gave one of the best shows of pure trick-flying that one has seen. Crazy flying in a Moth is more effective than on a bigger machine because it is so much quicker in movement, apart from its loops and spins which were unusually neat.' He went on: 'There was talk of holding a race for women pilots but it did not come off. So we had no chance of seeing Newcastle's own aviatrix, Miss Connie Leathart, in the air, which was a pity for good judges say this sporting little lady looks like being as good as a good, mere male pilot.' That turned out to be the case, for when World War II broke out, Connie joined the Auxiliary Air Transport command and ferried around all kinds of war planes. Today, an octogenarian, she lives alone with a life-time of memories in her farm at Little Bavington in Northumberland.

One of the characters of the very early days of the flying club at Cramlington was Arthur George, a Newcastle motor-trader and a founder member. He was very much a trail-blazer in light aeroplane flying, having won his licence elsewhere before Newcastle Aero Club was formed. J.D. remembers him well, though by the time Jim had been appointed Chief Flying Instructor at Woolsington in 1951, Arthur George had turned seventy, though he still flew.

A remarkable story involving a marathon car drive is told about Arthur George during the turbulent days of the General Strike of 1926. The background to the tale involves the printing of certain national newspapers like the *Daily Graphic* and the *Sunday Times* in Newcastle in order to get round the strike-bound printing presses in London. Newcastle Aero Club agreed to fly these newspapers to London for the duration of the strike. The local aeroplanes could not carry all the print run, so Arthur George motored down to Fleet St frequently, with his car full of newspapers. His astounding record run from Newcastle to London overnight carrying a load of newspapers hot off the presses in his '98 Vauxhall saloon car was six hours and thirteen minutes. For part of he journey he drove through driving rain. Just to show the mettle of his car, he motored back to Newcastle the same day.

Another character of the club and also a founder member was Philip Forsyth Heppell. He started his business life with his own company of estate agents, and later joined forces with Lamb and Edge of Newcastle. Heppell always reckoned that he was lucky to be alive after crash-landing behind German lines during the First World War. Attacked by enemy fighters, he was shot through the knee and forced down. When his plane landed he found that his severe wound prevented him leaving the cockpit of the plane—despite finding himself under fire from his own artillery! He thought that his time had come. Only the gallant action of a German soldier saved him: the German ran from the shelter of his trench towards the machine and pulled Heppell from the cockpit, carrying him to safety.

One amusing anecdote from the 1920s concerned a local flier, Samuel Smith Jnr. Out on a solo flight, he lost his bearings in fog and bad weather and had no option but to try and land in a farmer's field in County Durham. Unfortunately, during landing a wing caught the top of a wall turning the plane over in the farmyard. During the last few seconds before the crash, a startled farmer's wife saw the aeroplane hurtling towards her. As the machine struck the ground, the pilot was catapulted from his cockpit into a sludge farm carrying the woman with him in the process. Amazingly, the pair escaped serious injury though the smell was intolerable! The aeroplane, which had taken off from the club's airfield at Cramlington, was completely wrecked. The crash happened at Glebe Farm, Medomsley.

Moving on a decade, into the thirties, a dashing young airman called Leslie Runciman put the Newcastle Club on the national air race map when he won the prized Siddely Trophy in a race at Brooklands. Runciman, who lived at 'Doxford', Chathill, Northumberland, epitomised the flying 'bloods' of the day: dark, handsome and athletic-looking and always eager to race and compete. He won the Siddely for being the first club-trained pilot past the winning post in the King's Cup race. His machine was a DH Puss Moth G-ABLG powered by a Gypsy series III engine, average speed 130 m.p.h.

It was while he was at Cramlington that he and Connie Leathart established the Cramlington Aircraft Company. Later, he created and commanded the well-known No. 607 County of Durham Squadron of the Royal Auxiliary Air Force from 1930-1938. His achievements in airmanship won him the Air Force Cross in 1937. Leslie Runciman fought hard to establish the place of British aviation in the emerging new world of passenger-carrying by air. His appointments to the Boards of Imperial and British Airways, and his elevation to the Director-General of the British Overseas Aircraft Corporation gave him the platform to speak out. The ill-health of his father after the war caused him to give increased commitment to the family shipping business. On the death of his father he became Viscount Runciman of Doxford. He was appointed OBE in 1946 and Deputy-Lieut. of Northumberland in 1961. The elder son of Walter Runciman, the national Liberal statesman, Lord Runciman died in September, 1989 at the age of 89.

The year 1935 marked a turning point when the Newcastle Club, having outgrown its facilities at Cramlington, was ready to accept the management of the new Newcastle Airport at Woolsington. Soon the Civil Air Guard was formed, followed by the RAFVR and flying training increased accordingly until the beginning of the Second World War. Then all machines belonging to the flying club were requisitioned and private flying ceased.

Many club members were to distinguish themselves during World War II including Whaley Heppell, one of the 'Flying Heppells' of Newcastle

Aero Club. Whaley learned to fly with the RAFVR at Woolsington in 1939 and went on for further training at an RAF Station in Yorkshire prior to his posting with a war-time squadron. He flew with Douglas Bader in the Battle of Britain, won the DFC and Bar and later the Croix de Guerre. He became President of the Aero Club. He was a senior partner in Lamb and Edge, Newcastle, and died in 1989.

Also serving in that war was Philip Heppell, Whaley's father, now a Squadron Leader, and also J.D. Irving, a pillar of the Aero Club. A flier who made his mark was Squadron Leader James Rush. Another Squadron Leader was Bill Evans, the Chief Flying Instructor at Woolsington when war broke out.

Jim Denyer arrived on the North East scene during war-time, and as a Sgt. Pilot was stationed at RAF Ouston. Little could he have known when he had cause to visit RAF Woolsington that he was to spend all his working life there. After the war was over, he departed from Newcastle but only after having forged a lifetime link, marrying Mary Graham from Heaton. Commissioned, he spent the next six years as a RAF peace-time pilot.

Looking back on the achievements of Newcastle Aero Club in the world of air racing and competition, the golden era spanned the 1920s to the late 1950s. The club house honours boards tell their own stories of pilots who emerged victorious after tight, gruelling races and thrilling finishes. Names of old Aero Club pilots flying out of Cramlington evoke memories of the earliest days of light aeroplane flying.

Dr Hubert Dixon has pride of place on the first honours board, winning numerous air races from 1926 onwards. He was one of a number of crack local pilots who joined with leading national fliers to give demonstrations of flying in the twenties and thirties at Cramlington. In those days, the Air Pageants drew large crowds from all over Tyneside. Dr Dixon's biggest win was the British Aircraft Constructors' Challenge Cup, against all comers in 1929.

The club's flying instructor, J.D. Parkinson also had considerable success in air racing in 1926 and 1927, though as a professional pilot he had a head start. 'Parky', as he was known always recognised the role of his ground engineer, K.C. Brown in acknowledging his victories.

Other Newcastle pilots who proved outstanding winners in the early years of the Aero Club included Freddie Turnbull (at Birmingham), Norman Todd and Howard Phillips (Lancashire races), G.S. Kemp (National Air Races) and J.D. Irving , the man who was to play a leading role in the Newcastle Club's future (at Sherburn-in-Elmet). With the arrival of the thirties, Freddie Turnbull again demonstrated his flying skills by winning the Grosvenor Challenge Cup at a national meeting.

The local Aero Club did not receive the news gladly when J.D. Parkinson announced that he was leaving Newcastle to take up a post overseas. He was succeeded by F.P.J. McGevor as Flying Instructor at Cramlington. He too won air racing honours in both 1933 and 1934.

One of the outstanding woman pilots of the day, Winifred Brown, did not come from Newcastle, but she was the inaugural winner of the Aero Club's magnificent and most valuable trophy. This pre-eminent Mancunian and competition pilot, who had received the Newcastle upon Tyne Air Trophy, was the only woman to win the King's Cup.

The Newcastle Aero Club made great strides in the thirties but when war broke out in 1939, private flying at Woolsington ceased for six years. In the post-war years, one shining star to emerge in club flying was P.W.E. (Whaley) Heppell DFC who had distinguished himself as a war-time fighter pilot. He won members' races in 1948 and 1949. He was followed by Sqn/Ldr. W.M. Evans, AFC ( a pre-war club flying instructor) who won the Yorkshire Trophy in 1950. In the same year, K.C. Millican was victorious in the Grosvenor Trophy.

But the two pilots responsible for an impressive run of success in the fifties were Jim Denyer and Geoff Knox. During that time J.D.'s name appears on the Honours' Boards nine times under the heading of National Air Races. His achievements in air racing has been chronicled in an earlier chapter, and his record of winning two King's Cups from three starts is unlikely to be equalled.

Although Geoff Knox never won that top award, he was another first-class pilot. His successes in air racing and competition included winning the Royal Aero Club International Trophy in 1954, the Air League Cup in 1956, and the Osram Cup in 1956. During the 1950s, when the Flying Club was fighting to survive financially, the rates for flying in the Tiger Moths and Auster aircraft were pitched at dual flying: £3 5s. per hour, solo flying: £2 10s. per hour

They may seem infinitesimal sums compared with the £70 odd per hour charged today, but in the fifties, a good wage was around £10 per week, which puts the flying charges into perspective. During this time, the School purchased a Link Trainer from Carlisle which could be hired for 15s. per hour, and on bad flying days could be used for instrument training procedures. Unfortunately, this machine became frequently unserviceable and had to be sold off after only two years. For the more enthusiastic flying member, the Club purchased a twin-engined Gemini aircraft.

It was in 1952 that a Contract of Agreement was signed between the Aero Club and Newcastle Corporation, thus creating the first municipal flying school in England. While the Corporation, through J.D., organised flying facilities and operated the aircraft, the Aero Club supervised all social activities. A brochure of the day announced the creation of 'The Newcastle Municipal Flying School and Air Centre' and the attractions of flying from the Woolsington airfield. 'The Northumberland coast-line, which is noted for its beauty, affords pleasant and interesting flights on sunny days...' Trumpeting the arrival at Woolsington of the Link Trainer the brochure stated 'It does everything an aircraft can do without leaving the ground.' The brochure announced that the Club's annual subscription was four guineas and that half-hour flying lessons could also be taken for £1 17s. 6d.

By 1959, the Municipal Flying School had announced a new set of charges: Tiger Moth and Auster: Dual per hour £3 15s.; solo per hour £3 5s. Miles Gemini: Dual per hour £6 10s; solo per hour £5 15s.

In addition the School offered a number of services including charter aircraft (short and long distance) and a towing service. The 1959 handbook states: 'Since 1952, the School's engineering facility has prepared Woolsington aircraft for national competition, winning numerous honours.' Apart from maintaining and servicing club machines, the engineering staff also looked after privately-owned planes including the popular DH Rapides and Doves of that era. It was also during the late fifties that local pilot, Stan Jours hit the headlines in the national air races, winning the Kemsley Trophy first time out. Another Newcastle flier who met with success was Dr J.F. McClory, the club doctor, who won the Swiss International Air Rally. 'Mac' as he was known to one and all was a member of a small consortium who bought and flew a Percival Prentice aircraft and later a Proctor machine.

Throughout the years, Newcastle Aero Club has produced many fine pilots, some of whom were characters. One such flier is Piercy Dixon, who for some years was a publican, running the Cheviot public house at Bellingham.

Outside of flying circles, few people were aware that Piercy flew a medical spare-parts emergency service, using his own aircraft to fly life-saving missions up and down the country. Organised by St John's Ambulance Air Wing, London, the service was directed from an operations centre at Epsom. Mr Dixon was and still is the Northern Co-ordinator for the service. In addition, for seven years, he acted as a volunteer pilot to fly medical spare parts—mostly hearts and kidneys—for major operations and surgery all over the country. He also ferried special drugs when called for in an emergency. It was a labour of love for Piercy; there was no pay, just fuel expenses were refunded. Speed was of the essence in flying this emergency service. One minute Piercy would be serving behind the bar at his Bellingham pub, the next minute, after a phone call from the London or Epsom Air Wing, he would be on his way to Newcastle Airport to jump into his own plane for a quick take off. Sometimes he was accompanied by his friend, Bill Knox Haggie who had an interest in the attractive aircraft they flew, G-AYXX ('Double X Ray') which was a single engine Cessna and a joy to fly.

Often emergency calls would come to Mr Dixon at night in bad weather. He had a few risky trips though the worst involved flying special drugs into Belfast Harbour in a winter storm. In view of the ferocious conditions, the airport had been closed earlier that night. It was re-opened especially to accept Piercy Dixon who was battling through low cloud, poor visibility and driving rain. Brought into land by radar, he delivered his valuable load before succumbing to exhaustion and sleep.

Apart from flying the medical spare parts service, Mr Dixon was a keen competitor in air rallies, especially during the 1970s and early 1980s. Twice he was chosen as a member of the British Team which competed in the International Air Rally Championship.

The late Bob Costella, of Darras Hall, Ponteland, was the longest-serving member of the Aero Club (joining in 1938) and this was recognised some time ago when he was made an Honorary Life Member. One of the characters of the club, he served on the Committee for some years during the 1950s. He once owned a lovely little aeroplane called the Signet, the first aircraft to be manufactured with a tricycle under-carriage. Bob Costella remembered the financial crisis that hit flying operations at the Aero Club in the 1950s, when there was talk about the possibility of flying folding up within a year or so. The fact was that Aero Clubs generally have never been great commercial success stories, and this period, with the nation still suffering the economic aftermath of World War II, was particularly difficult.

By this time J.D., former Chief Flying Instructor at the Club, had become Commandant of the Airport and he was determined that club flying should not fail. It is thanks to him that flying was not interrupted. He persuaded Newcastle Corporation to take over the Flying School—a move that was not universally acclaimed by City Councillors, some of them objecting to the extra loading on the ratepayers of Newcastle.

For the first year under new management the flying side of the club continued to lose money, though within two years broke even. By 1960 the flying club was restored to full health and had made a piece of civil flying history by becoming the first Municipal Flying School. The Aero Club, more than grateful for J.D.'s support, then assumed management once again.

Another landmark in the club's history coincided with the opening of the new airport at Woolsington in 1967. After nearly twenty years in 'temporary accommodation' behind the large hangar, the club returned to its pre-war home. Members were pleased to return to their inviting brick building headquarters which, after extension and modernisation (complete with restaurant) was and is one of the best club houses. There was an enthusiastic buzz around the place, mirroring the big upsurge among people wanting to learn to fly. In 1967 alone, more than 2,000 hours were logged instructing pupil pilots. In that year the social side and the flying side came closer together. On a sunny afternoon members could arrive at the club, and with every facility at their elbow watch the flying going on around them.

One of the hidden secrets of the history of Newcastle Aero Club can now be told. A wealthy group of business operators who had moved into the North East from the London area made a bold move to take over the Aero Club building and turn it into a night club. Jim Denyer was horrified to hear the news. 'An entity of that kind operating on an airfield with access to the air side of the operation would have been a great hazard, and hardly the kind of thing to be associated with a growing international airport,' he said. The problem was that the take-over group, who had night club interests in Newcastle as well as the marketing and operation of the new fruit machine business, had made a handsome offer to the Airport Committee of Newcastle City Council for the Aero Club building. The records show that this outside offer was many more times than the Aero Club could afford to pay, and was without doubt tempting. J.D. was strongly opposed to the Aero Club losing its building and spoke out against the offer. The result was that the offer was rejected.

During the 'Swinging Sixties' international cabaret stars often appeared in Newcastle night clubs. One singing star, Mel Torme, already an enthusiast of light aeroplane flying in America, asked J.D. to teach him to fly the Tiger Moth during an engagement in Newcastle. Like thousands of others, Torme had fallen in love with the Moth. For a beginner, the Tiger was not the easiest plane to fly and Torme's flying lessons coincided with a period of wild and stormy weather. Nevertheless the instructions were a success, as a result of which Torme and J.D. became friends.

During the fifties, J.D. and the Newcastle flying school staff treated their precious Tiger Moths with great care. J.D. looked back with nostalgia and a heavy heart to the day when Newcastle Corporation sold off the machines at 'give away' prices. In those days, Moths could be disposed of for as little as £200. Today, an air-worthy Tiger Moth in first-class condition can fetch as much as £30,000. 'I nearly cried when the Tiger Moths flew out of Newcastle for the last time, but by then the more modern Auster aircraft were in demand,' he said. The 'Tiggie', which trained hundreds of RAF pilots during World War II made its appearance in 1931 as the de Havilland DH 60 T, noteworthy for its staggered wings. (The prototype Moth, the DH 51 was designed in 1924 though, because of engine limitations, it was not taken up by flying clubs. It took another seven years for the Tiger Moth to appear).

It was the DH 60 with the first reliable aero-engine, the Cirrus which launched the light aeroplane movement. Three years later de Havilland introduced the DH 60G which made an impact with its improved Gypsy engine. The DH 80A, designed in 1930 and known as the Puss Moth featured an advanced closed cockpit; and then in 1933, Sir Geoffrey de Havilland won the King's Cup air race flying his Leopard Moth. It is generally accepted that over the years, some 9,000 Tiger Moths were built but it seems no one knows the precise figure. It is estimated that today more than 500 still survive, one or two in the north, many in good flying condition. They are spread all over the world. J.D. always said: 'If you can fly a Tiger well, you can fly anything.' Pupils could not fool around with a Tiger—it was intolerant of sloppy handling but J.D. always had a soft spot for the machine.

As the years went on, Newcastle Aero Club went from strength to strength winning much prestige in the flying club movement. By 1968 the club membership had risen to nearly 700 and today stands at over 1,000. Also in 1968 the British Light Aviation movement honoured Newcastle with a Seminar which attracted more than 200 people from different parts of the country. Meeting with the Light Aviation Centre and the Guild of Air Pilots and Navigators was the General Aviation Safety Council. Organising the event was Alan Summers, an Aero Club pilot taught by J.D. and the joint owner of a twin engine Gemini (with John Lewis).

The club celebrated its forty-fifth birthday in 1970 with an 'Open Day' which attracted hundreds of visitors to Woolsington. Jimmy Logan, the entertainer, himself a pilot, officially opened the event.

The next step forward for the Club was the purchase of a flight simulator used for training with an instructor.

The major event of 1974 was an international air rally, organised by the club and to which pilots from all over Europe were invited. By this time Newcastle Airport was a hive of activity as well as the Aero Club. All this busy air traffic, particularly in the summer months was confined to a single runway! With so many movements there could have been a real problem for Woolsington; in the event there was none. To make life easier all round, J.D. introduced a system of varying circuits. It sounds simple enough, as the best solutions always are. Club pilots conformed with the following procedure: taking off to the west they flew right-hand circuits to keep them north; taking off to the east they did left-hand circuits, again to keep them north. Thus the south of the airfield, the approach for the large commercial passenger carrying aircraft, was kept clear. To fly this single runway under such traffic conditions, flying club pilots had to be good. They had to fly integrated schedules with airline passenger planes which were given priority on landing and take-off. They had to be conversant with aircraft radio techniques, also capable of cross-wind landings and fully efficient on instrument flying. 'When a pupil learned his flying skills at Newcastle, he was one of the highest-trained private pilots in the country' said J.D.

Private flying, like much else in aviation has changed significantly in the last forty years. Jim recalled the early 1950s when he was instructing at Woolsington. You flew in either Tiger Moths or Austers; there was a minimum of navigational aids and radios were nowhere to be seen. 'Today's light aircraft are more sophisticated machines with smart navigational aids, advanced radios, and tricycle undercarriages...the types of aircraft and flying itself has changed substantially in the last forty years. Procedures have changed, discipline has been tightened up and radio working efficiency is mandatory for all private pilots. Aircraft movements on grassy areas were abandoned in 1967—and all traffic switched to the airport's single runway...on the whole, flying club operations work well, although you might get the odd complaint from club pilots who taxi out and are held for twenty minutes because four aircraft are landing and three are taking off. The situation has been eased by the opening of the parallel taxi-way.'

One of the main changes in the world of light aeroplane flying has been the rocketing cost of learning to fly. When J.D. was Chief Flying Instructor at Newcastle the flying charges were £2 10s. solo and £3 5s. dual, and the instructor got half the difference—that was 7s. 6d. then or 37p in today's money! To learn to fly in the 1990s costs in the region of £70 per hour, which means that the average pupil has to invest some £600 on flying lessons before going solo. 'Though the yearning to fly remains, and more pupils keep coming along to learn, including many young people.'

J.D. was rightly proud of the progress in aviation made by pupils taught by him. One such local pilot, Mike Gill, opted for a flying spell with the Royal Air Force after which he returned to Woolsington as an instructor. When Mike quit to launch what became Gill Aviator, Services, then Gill Air, freelance instructors were used for a while until the Club once again resumed full responsibility for instructing pupil pilots. Gill Air is a flourishing schedule flying airline at Newcastle in 1993, though under new owners.

One club stalwart and private flier, whom J.D. worked alongside for many years is Fred Knight, a former Aero Club secretary and treasurer, and in later years Club chairman until 1992. Fred, too, has witnessed major changes in private flying in the last twenty years. When he joined the club, only two machines were available; over the years that gradually built up until in 1992 the club owned six aircraft.

Although the club is financially sound today, it was not always so—Fred can recall earlier times when club members dug into their own pockets to provide funds to purchase aeroplanes. Then, as the club sailed into healthier financial waters, the club was able to pay back the members. An indication of a thriving Aero Club is the increase in flying hours over the year, from 2000 hours per year when Fred joined until more than 4,500 hours in 1992. When Sunderland Flying Club closed down some years ago, many members transferred to Woolsington. There has been a sea change in the kind of people who come to Woolsington to learn to fly today. Mr Knight remembers that years ago, members were drawn largely from the business people of Tyneside. Now, a broad cross-section of society is learning to fly; pupil pilots include taxi drivers, joiners, electricians, students as well as business people. Not that training to become a pilot is cheap. In 1992, it is reckoned that on average it costs around £3,000 for a person to be trained to the peak of acquiring a licence. These days, some would-be fliers think nothing of taking out a loan to meet the cost of training.

Fred Knight—chairman at the time of writing—looking back over the years at the history of the club is only too well aware of the part played by Jim Denyer for four decades. In the fifties he kept the Aero Club's planes flying when there was a threat of a shut-down. With the Aero Club grappling with financial problems J.D., as Commandant of Newcastle Airport and previous CFI of the Aero Club persuaded Newcastle Corporation to come to the rescue. 'Without his help, the club would have found it extremely difficult to continue,' said Fred. 'Through the years he has given other help, including protection of the exclusive status of the flying school ... The great love in the life of Jim has been flying. I've flown with him many times, a born pilot and outstanding instructor. He changed completely once he sat in the cockpit of an aeroplane, gone was the mantle of the managing director, replaced by a courteous, skillful pilot, a joy to fly with. He loved Newcastle Aero Club—we shall always be in his debt ... There are also many people on Tyneside whom he helped without others knowing. As a friend for many years, I can say that although Jim appeared to be something of a crusty character on the outside, underneath there was a heart of gold.'

Although flying light aeroplanes is the function of any aero club, the provision of first-class engineering services and good club facilities for members must come a close second. Newcastle aero engineers have through the year ranked among the best in the country; and since the 1960s, when the club-house was modernised and extended, the Newcastle Aero Club has been recognised as possessing one of the best aero club headquarters in the UK. Through the years, succeeding club committees have maintained that reputation; the club-house was further enhanced in 1974 when an extension of the club and bar areas took place. Today's committees have continued that enterprise, with new improvements introduced in the early 1990s, including the provision of a new lounge area. For some years now, the management of the club bar and restaurant has been in the capable hands of Beryl and Rennie Alexander.

Any successful club should be more than grateful to those members prepared to give their time and expertise to serve on committees. Fred

Knight, a long-standing member has already been mentioned; after yeoman service as club chairman, he retired in June, 1992. Another stalwart, Bob Shanks, retired at the same time. Bill Knox Haggie served on the committee for many years and in 1993 was elected President. Others who should be mentioned include Mrs Eve Irvine, Norman Wilson and Dr J.F.M. McClory. The late George Barker, a Tyneside businessman, helped the Aeroclub through its financial difficulties in the 1950s. Milton Beattie has been the club secretary for some years, though he first joined as a member twenty years ago. He is the centre of a little piece of club history himself—he is the only living member of the club to have flown on the opening day of Newcastle Airport in 1935. Taken to Woolsington on the big day as a five-year-old, he can recall that the Alan Cobham Flying Circus was offering joy rides at 7s. 6d. a time. 'I was taken up by a relative and can still recall the thrill of flying over Tyneside at 2,000 feet as a small boy all those years ago.'

It should not be forgotten that for some years, Newcastle Airport was efficiently run by leaders of the Aero Club until eventually, Newcastle Corporation took over the management. And although Jim set a record as the longest-serving President of the Club, he was well aware of the pre-eminent contributions made to the office by his predecessors in the 1920s and 1930s and the ensuing decades. Men like Sir Joseph Reed, John Boyd, J.D. Irving and Whaley Heppell.

Before we know it—in 1995—Newcastle Aero Club will be celebrating its seventieth birthday. Although maturing into a septuagenarian by then, that is not to say it won't continue to go from strength to strength. Light aeroplane club flying has been established firmly at Woolsington for many years now, and has made its mark throughout the country and even in northern France. Today's buzzing atmosphere at Newcastle, with a hive of activity around the tarmac and airfield is a far cry from the small beginnings on an old flying field at Cramlington. Since that time, the Aero Club has prospered to become one of the most prestigious club organisations on Tyneside, a pillar of private flying in the North East region.

Where Newcastle led the way all those years ago, other clubs were soon to follow. What Cramlington, and then Woolsington did for flying was to open up aviation opportunities for the average man or woman of moderate means. You didn't have to be a millionaire to fly at Newcastle. The facilities afforded by the Aero Club made it possible for a formidable band of Geordie private pilots to emerge with licences in the inter-war years. When World War II broke out, it was bands of pilots like those from Tyneside who were first into uniform—to join the professional pilots of the RAF squadrons. But wars are also the enemy of all civil flying clubs, as invariably they are closed down for the duration and, like a phoenix, struggle to rise from the ashes once hostilities are over.

Newcastle flying club in peace-time has that ideal location which features beautiful countryside, the coastline and the sea. The joy of flying down the Northumberland coastline on a balmy day amid sunny blue skies has to be experienced to be believed. In the early days it must have been heaven: strapped in the open cockpit of the DH Moth, being pushed forward by the straight-four Cirrus engine, pleasingly buffeted by air currents in empty skies with the cool wind blowing on the cheeks. Light aeroplane flying is still vastly enjoyable though the silence is shattered by the staccato radio calls, and the once empty skies are crowded now. The private pilot has to take his chance with the wide-bodied transatlantic jet aircraft which fly in and out of Woolsington.

The decades of private flying in Newcastle could not have taken place without the inspiring first steps taken by the pioneers of 1925. The tiny band of founder members were joined at the start of the thirties by such stalwarts as J.D. Irving, Freddie Turnbull, Dr Eric Dagger and N.S. Todd. J.D. Irving, who ran a Rolls Royce limousine, was affectionately known as 'Rockefeller' by members. At that time, the club proudly described itself as: 'The Newcastle upon Tyne Aero Club Ltd, Cramlington Aerodrome, Northumberland, Telephone—Cramlington 9.' A club handbook of the time reveals a number of illustrious names among the list of vice-presidents: Lt. Col. Clifton Brown M.P. (who became Speaker of the House of Commons); Viscount Ridley; Col. W.M. Angus; and Sir Alan Cobham, KBE, AFC.

From the outset, flying clubs throughout the country have never yielded handsome profits, but although Newcastle has flown through financial turbulence from time to time, it has always managed to emerge to make a safe landing. It must be gratifying for members, as they look back over nearly seventy years of private flying, to reflect on the initiative of Newcastle and four other centres to begin and establish aero clubs. That example was quickly followed by the rest of the country, and then by the dominions and colonies of the British Empire. Long before the outbreak of World War II, light aeroplane flying clubs—modelled on the British pattern—had been set up throughout the world. The appetite for this new phenomenon of aviation was such that almost overnight many thousands of would-be aviators were having their first experience at the controls of a flying machine. With hindsight, it can be stated without fear of contradiction that their contribution to the advancement of civil aviation has been immense.

In the 1990s Newcastle upon Tyne Aero Club continues to occupy a leading position among the flying clubs of Great Britain. Headquartered at Woolsington, the club exhibits the same vitality and enterprise that have characterised it from the beginning. No one can say that the Club motto, coined at Cramlington in 1925, has not been fulfilled: 'By your own efforts shall ye Rise.'

# Postscript

## THE DEMISE OF DAN-AIR

Since the completion of this book an event has taken place at Newcastle which demands to be described in full, as it forms an important part of airport history with strong links with J.H. Denyer.

When the last Dan-Air flight took off from Woolsington on the evening of Monday, 2 November 1992, it was the closing chapter of an airline which played a leading part in the development of domestic and foreign services at Newcastle. Furthermore, it was J.D. who was largely responsible for Davies and Newman, a London firm of shipping brokers launching out into the aviation business. That Company entered aviation almost by accident. Back in 1953, Davies and Newman were landed with a Dakota aircraft which they received as part of a debt, and Fred Newman, one of the partners was at a loss to know what to do with it. As it happened, J.D. knew Fred Newman and when the Dakota was flown into Newcastle, he said words to the effect, 'I just don't know what to do with the thing.' The response from J.D. was, 'Why don't you operate it?' In those few seconds the suggestion hit home and thus was an air-line born, 'Dan-Air' taking its name from the initial letters of the parent company. Its full title was 'Dan-Air Services'.

During the next thirty years, the Airline became a nucleus of the development of scheduled services from Newcastle to destinations both home and abroad; it grew up alongside Newcastle and forged a permanent bond between pilots, air stewardesses, operational and terminal staff. While other national carriers passed Newcastle by, Dan-Air, although originally based at Southend before switching to Gatwick, established a base at Woolsington, locating some of its aircraft here and gradually building up its staff members.

In the teething troubles of the early years, when its fleet included numbers of second-hand mature aircraft it was initially dubbed 'Dan-Dare' by a few disgruntled passengers, though as the airline prospered and bought new aeroplanes, it became known as the friendly airline at Newcastle and 'Dan-Dare' remained only as an affectionate nickname. Although in its first few years the airline was engaged in only charter operations which included Southend to Shannon, and a Government freight contract to Singapore, in 1954 the company bought a second Dakota which was used to transport ships' crews around Europe; and the following year more aircraft were bought to fly cargo to Africa and the Far East. In 1956 the carrier launched its first scheduled passenger service, from

Blackbushe Airport to Jersey. By 1960, Dan-Air had forged a link with Newcastle on its West Country service from Bristol which took in Manchester and Liverpool on its flight north, operating de Havilland Doves. The same year, the company launched its first international service from the west of England to Switzerland.

In the first ten years of operations, Dan-Air clocked up annual passenger figures of 100,000, and later was to carry more than 50,000 passengers to London, Gatwick alone. By 1971, the carrier was operating a 'Link City' service between Newcastle, Manchester, Bristol and Cardiff, flying the Nord 262 machines. Two years later Dan-Air had launched the Newcastle-London service, carrying smaller numbers of passengers but competing successfully against the giant carrier, British Airways which flew frequent daily flights into Heathrow. By this time, Dan-Air had bought BAC I-II pure jets to supplement their Comet fleet, replacing the faithful Ambassador / Elizabethans. The airline was by this time well established, prospering and employing first-class professional staff. In 1974, they opened up the Newcastle-Jersey route, a popular service for holiday-makers from the North East region; and the next year launched scheduled services into Scandinavia, a shrewd move linking the two countries geographically opposite one another and only separated by water. Bergen and Kristiansand first linked up with Newcastle, to be followed in later years by Oslo and Stavanger. The airline was on its toes and always looking for new business. When in August 1974 tour operators were shocked by the Court Line crash, Dan-Air was one of the carriers which began an airlift for nearly 50,000 tourists stranded overseas.

By 1980 the Dan-Air fleet had grown to some forty aircraft with a turnover of around £100,000,000. Over the years, the airline has operated twenty-five scheduled destinations and twenty holiday destinations from Newcastle, more than any other carrier. During that time it had established a popular run to Amsterdam, and domestically had run scheduled flights into centres like Belfast, Dublin and Aberdeen. So what were the hammer blows that nailed this airline to the runway, eventually killing it off? Aviation commentators blamed the deep-seated recession which was still creating economic havoc by the closing months of 1992. For some years, the airline had not been tremendously healthy financially, and had struggled in a very competitive market. At the best of times the aviation industry is highly cyclical, earnings are volatile and future capital requirements are always large. Re-equipping fleets with new, modern jets costs a fortune, and bottoms have to fall on seats to keep airlines viable. The airline was badly hit by the fall in the package holiday business, normally flying many charters for national tour operators. Dan-Air also found to their cost that in the last few years, the schedule routes they flew could not sustain competition from other airlines.

Jim Denyer was very sad to be told that Dan-Air was to fold up. He had many memories of the association. In 1985, the airline managers presented him with a beautiful model of the Hawker Siddely 146, four-engine jet, in company livery 'in appreciation of twenty-five years of co-operation from the manager of Newcastle Airport'. In 1992, some thirty-two years after first arriving at Woolsington, J.D. said of the airline: 'I am extremely sad to see Dan-Air go under, particularly an airline of their calibre which I have known from the beginning. They fostered and helped the development of scheduled services in Newcastle and the North East. They were a progressive airline company and tried very hard at everything they undertook.'

Through the years, Dan-Air had become the family airline at Newcastle Airport. It made the final departure all the more melancholy.

On a blustery, winter's evening on Monday 2 November 1992, a sombre scene was set. With a Scots Piper playing a lament, Dan-Air carrier, 'Smokey Joe', the twin engined jet of flight DA-107 prepared for take-off, destination—Gatwick, London. The mourners comprised the 100 or so staff who had worked on the company operation at Newcastle; the pilots, air stewardesses, reception and other staff who had worked their last day for Dan-Air, and faced a bleak future. A receptionist with seventeen years' service said: 'It's a big loss for the North East. Our regular passengers will be sorry to see us go.'

Captain Alan Stanford, piloting the last flight to Gatwick remarked: 'It's very sad. After operating this service for many years, its loss will hit a lot of people very hard.'

Thus the curtain fell on Dan-Air, the airline founded on a chance remark by Jim Denyer. The twin jets of Flight DA-107 lifted the aircraft off the Woolsington runway, thrusting it away for the last time after forty years in the aviation business. The machine disappeared into the pale sunset of a November evening, only to be gobbled up by a giant called British Airways.

# Appendix

## NEWCASTLE INTERNATIONAL AIRPORT—1993

Today's modern twentieth century Newcastle International Airport towers over the area as the jewel in the North East's crown. By enterprising management, it has sustained its position among the top dozen airports in the country, in 1993 taking over the number ten position.

New road, rail and metro links have created one of the most accessible airports in Europe. Newcastle has always taken pride in the facilities and speedy ground service provided for passengers; a policy that has yielded its reward in the huge increase in passengers in the last twenty-five years.

Record passenger traffic was recorded in the year 1991/92 with numbers approaching 1.7 million. In 1993 Newcastle topped 2 million passengers—a stark contrast to the 5,000 people who flew out of the airport in the early fifties. The major breakthrough in passenger traffic was made in the late sixties and seventies with the introduction of fully-inclusive holidays abroad. Holiday passengers from Newcastle have had an extended choice of destinations for many years now; by the nineties that choice included long-haul flights to North America. Today fifty destinations are available across three continents.

While scheduled services link Newcastle to ten international centres and ten UK airports including three London terminals, Heathrow, Gatwick, and Stansted, market research suggests a demand for additional scheduled services especially international. Airport staff are campaigning to link the region direct to influential European industrial, financial and business centres. Germany has been selected for special attention. A North East survey indicated a demand for regular services to places like Düsseldorf, Frankfurt, Copenhagen, Milan and Madrid. Such are the economics of the airline business that the 'new route factor' comes into play; no matter how well an airport sells and markets itself, airlines will not open up new routes unless they are convinced that they can make them profitable. Newcastle continues to strive to build up its direct European services. In the meantime the growth of passenger traffic goes on. Feasibility studies predict that this growth will continue, and that there will be a massive increase—doubling traffic shortly after the arrival of the new millennium. Extending the forecast further, it is predicted that 4,500,000 passengers will pass through Newcastle by the year 2007, a mere fourteen years away.

Such major growth will prompt considerable expansion to the airport complex. In the pipe-line are plans to push the concourse frontage outwards, followed by expansion to the north. Space will created by transferring all cargo operations to a purpose-built 'freight village' south of the terminal. Planning permission for this major project, costing nearly £5m. has been received and work got under way in 1993. An indication of the size of the freight business at Newcastle is the number of freight agents and forwarders on site, numbering fifteen. A new freight village will support the viability of scheduled services, with the spin-off of attracting new airlines to open up new routes from Woolsington.

The airport has been a hive of activity during recent years. By late 1992 a new rooftop extension, comprising fourteen offices and five executive lounges had been completed. One piece of enterprise was the airport's own 'Air Executive' business club, offering full business facilities for the industrialist and the businessman. The main executive area has been named 'The Denyer Suite', honouring the name of the man who did so much for Newcastle International Airport. Another initiative was a £2m. apron extension adding seven new aircraft stands (making nineteen in all). Increase in passengers and projected growth can be accommodated by an increase in the size of the apron by a third. Another new development in 1993 was the building of a new General Aviation Centre, the initiative of two businessmen who are both private pilots who formed 'Samsom Aviation Services'. This centre is dedicated to the needs of private and business aircraft, as well as offering a wide range of services. Work also took place in 1993 to expand the long-term car parking area. The new facility provided another 2,400 spaces taking the capacity to 3,400 cars.

So much for 1993. Looking into the future, major long-term developments include either the building of a free-standing pier for aircraft; or a new parallel pier which would be erected to the north of the existing one. Large sums of money are needed to implement these large-scale developments: a sum of £125m. is being talked about as the cost of expansion over the next fifteen years.

On the evidence of the past, the future looks to be secure. With passenger traffic in the region of 2 million annually, and with a net profit for 1991/92 nudging £3m., the local authority owners are determined to resist Government pressure to sell off Woolsington.

## KEY DATES IN THE HISTORY OF NEWCASTLE AIRPORT

1929    Newcastle City Council first discuss the idea of an airport.

1935    Newcastle Airport opens at Woolsington (Managers: Newcastle Aero Club).

1939-45 Taken over by the war-time Royal Air Force.

1946    Woolsington handed back by the RAF. (Managers: Newcastle Corporation).

1946-52 No scheduled services but charters and private flying.

1952    J.H. Denyer appointed Commandant. First schedule flights begin.

1963    Newcastle Corporation cease to hold authority over Airport. Formation of NE Regional Airport Committee.

1967    New Airport Terminal opened.

1978    Government Categorisation of Airports—Newcastle attains Regional Airport Status.

1982    Major Terminal expansion and other development.

1986    Government Airport Act.
        Newcastle becomes a private limited company.

1989    New Parallel Taxi-way opened.
        Jim Denyer retires after thirty-seven years' service at the Airport.

1991    Metro Rail link opened connecting the Airport to main line station at Newcastle upon Tyne.

1993    Major terminal expansion.
        Dedicated freight village.
        Extensions to apron and car parking capacity.

## FACTS AND FIGURES

Newcastle International Airport PLC stands on a 540 acre site six miles north west of Newcastle. The total share capital of this private limited company is held by the following authorities: Sunderland Metropolitan Borough Council; Newcastle City Council; Gateshead Metropolitan Borough Council; North Tyneside Metropolitan Borough Council; South Tyneside Metropolitan Borough Council; Durham County Council; and Northumberland County Council.

There are twenty-seven members of the Board of Directors including the airport managing director and his two deputies.

Chairman of the Board: Coun. J.A.P. Hattam
Deputy chairman: Coun. F. Long
Managing Director: C. Trevor Went
Director of Operations, G.K. Riddick
Finance and Commercial Director and Company Secretary, J. Bainbridge

Airport elevation: 266 feet above sea level
Main runway length: 2,332 metres. Width 46m
Terminal building: maximum annual through-put: over 2 million passengers
Identification Beacon: Flashing Green NE

TOTAL PASSENGERS HANDLED

| | |
|------|----------|
| 1951 | 5,300 |
| 1957 | 33,835 |
| 1960 | 119,098 |
| 1965 | 253, 955 |
| 1970 | 416, 766 |
| 1975 | 694,986 |
| 1980 | 1,027,411 |
| 1981 | 1,074,170 |
| 1988 | 1,500,000 |
| 1993 | 2,000,000 |

## ACKNOWLEDGEMENTS AND THANKS

Mary, Vivian and Michael Denyer

Newcastle International Airport: Alan Shaw (ATC), Mike Finch and Hilary Knox (Marketing and Press)
Newcastle Aero Club: Fred Knight, Bob Shanks, Bob Costella and Milton Beattie
Newcastle Central Library (Local History Department)
Northern Development Company
Tyne and Wear Archives, Newcastle

Lewis Benjamin (Tiger Club)
John Boyd, Gosforth
Dr Peter Burnett
Alan Taylor (ex-No. 29 Squadron, RAF.)
Rhoda Fairbairn, West Brunton, Gosforth
Connie Leathart, Little Bavington, Northumberland
Bill Wallace (Appleby Books, Morpeth)
Newcastle Chronicle and Journal Ltd, Northern Echo, Shields Gazette, Daily Telegraph, Sunday Times, News Chronicle


**Photographic Acknowledgements**

Air Fotos, Newcastle; Stewart Bonney, Newcastle; Boyd Archives; Denyer Archives; *Evening World*; Rhoda Fairbairn; *Flight International*; Harrison Photography, Newcastle; Hodder and Stoughton and the estate of Sheila Scott (photograph from *I Must Fly*); Sydney Johnson; Ian McFarlane; Dudley Muir; Newcastle Aero Club; Newcastle Chronicle & Journal Ltd; Newcastle International Airport; Newgate Studios, Stableford; *Northern Echo*; *Royal Aero Club Gazette*; Colin Simister, Darlington; *Sunderland Echo*; Colin Thompson; Turners Photography, Newcastle; Tom Weike, Copenhagen; David West; Geoffrey Willey, Ponteland; E.K. Woolcott, Southend.


Newcastle City Libraries & Arts gratefully acknowledge the support of Newcastle International Airport.

## BIBLIOGRAPHY

Bramson, Alan
and Birch, Neville
*The Tiger Moth Story* (Cassell, 1964)

Brownhill, Annette
*The Resource Workbook of Newcastle Airport*
(Newcastle City Library, 1981)

Dan-Air
*Silver Jubilee Anniversary* (Newcastle City
Library, 1978)

Endres, Gunter
*British Civil Aviation* (Ian Allen, London, 1985)

Middlebrook, Sydney
*Newcastle upon Tyne. Its Growth and
Achievements* ( The Journal)

Newcastle Airport
*Fifty Years* 1935-1985 (Newcastle City Library)

Rawnsley C.F.
and Wright, Robert
*Night Fighter* (Collins, 1957)

Rodrigo, Robert
*Berlin Airlift* (Cassell and Co., 1960)

Tapper, Oliver
*Armstrong Whitworth Aircraft Since 1913* (Putnam,
1973)


## OFFICIAL REPORTS

North of England
Regional Consortium
*Statement of case against Stansted* (City Library
1982)

NE Regional Airport
Committee
*Report of Chief Officers of Tyne and Wear County
Council and Durham C.C. with Airport Manager*
(City Library 1974)

Snow, Sir Frederick
and Partners
*Study for Future Expansion* (City Library 1971)

Snow, Sir Frederick
and Partners
*Survey of Terminal Users* (City Library 1972)

Snow, Sir Frederick     *Terminal Building Expansion* (City Library 1978)
and Partners

Snow, Sir Frederick     *Northern Region Airport Study* (CAA Papers 1978)
and Partners
and Stamp Associates

Stratford, Alan     *Report for Civil Aviation Authority—1975.*

Government White     *Airports Policy* (Cmnd 7084, 1978)
Paper

Civil Aviation     *Future Airport Development in North Region* (City
Authority     Library 1975)

Government Statistical     *Regional Trends 24* (Aviation Tables for Regions
Service     1989)

HMSO     *The Airport Act—1986, Airports Policy—1985*

(Note: City Library sources refer to the Local Studies Section of Newcastle
Central Library)

© John Sleight, 1993